WHEN HEARTS GROW HARD

- *Hidden Reason Marriages Break Down*

Healing the Heart Through Matthew 19:8

By

Mike Olorogun

Epigraph

"Because of the hardness of your hearts…"

— Matthew 19:8

Disclaimer

The names, characters, and situations used in this book are fictitious and are intended for illustrative purposes only. Any resemblance to actual persons, living or deceased, is purely coincidental. The stories are designed to teach, inspire, and provide practical guidance for couples and should not be taken as real-life accounts.

Table of Contents

Dedication

To every couple standing in the tension between covenant and conflict.

To every heart that still dares to hope.

To every marriage fighting to breathe again, longing for renewal and restoration.

This book is written for you- may its words be a light on your path and a witness to God's faithfulness.

Foreword

Marriage rarely collapses in a single moment—it fractures gradually, often silently, and always spiritually. What begins as small cracks in communication or neglected tenderness can, over time, harden hearts and erode intimacy. Jesus diagnosed this reality in Matthew 19:8 when He said, "Because of the hardness of your hearts…" In that profound statement, He revealed that the true battle in marriage is not external but internal, rooted in the condition of the heart.

When Hearts Grow Hard is a timely and necessary statement for couples in every season of life. It does not shy away from the sobering truth that marriages drift when hearts grow cold, but it also proclaims the hope that God restores. Within the pages of this book, you will find both diagnosis and prescription: why hearts harden, how intimacy fades, and how God's Spirit can soften, renew, and rebuild what has been broken.

As a pastor, I have witnessed both the pain of fractured marriages and the beauty of restored ones. I have walked with couples through valleys of bitterness and resentment, only to see them discover that God's grace is greater than their failures. This book is not about blame—it is about redemption. It is a call to return to God's blueprint, to reclaim covenant love, and to allow your marriage to become a living testimony of His faithfulness.

Whether you are newly married, facing trials in your marriage, or seeking renewal after years of struggle in your union, the truths contained here will guide you toward healing and covenantal alignment. Read it with an open heart, ready to let God soften what has grown hard, and may your marriage shine as a witness of His enduring love.

Pastoral Blessing:

May the Lord, the Author and Sustainer of covenant love, guard your hearts and guide your steps. May His Spirit soften what has grown hard, heal what has been wounded, and restore what has been broken. May your marriage reflect His faithfulness, becoming a living testimony of grace, unity, and resilience. And may every page of this book draw you closer to His divine blueprint, so that your love endures, your covenant thrives, and your union glorifies God for generations to come.

"When hearts grow hard, God's love grows stronger—restoring covenant, renewing intimacy, and redeeming what was broken."

Prologue

From Warning to Restoration

Before vows were spoken and rings exchanged, there were warnings. God whispered through His Spirit. Parents offered counsel. Mentors shared wisdom. The heart itself stirred with caution. Yet too often, those voices were silenced or ignored. Many rushed into marriage carried by romance, attraction, or urgency, believing that love alone would be enough. Feelings were mistaken for foundation, passion was assumed to be proof, and timing was dismissed as irrelevant.

In my earlier book, *Think Before You Say "I Do"*, we explored the importance of preparation, discernment, and heart work before entering marriage. That book was a guide to prevention—a roadmap for building wisely, asking the hard questions, and aligning with God's design before stepping into covenant. It was a call to pause, to prepare, and to protect the sacredness of marriage before saying yes.

Yet even with preparation, many couples still falter. Some dismissed advice. Some overlooked incompatibilities. Some silenced the still, small voice of God. Others began well but failed to heed His counsel in real time, allowing preventable problems to grow unchecked. The result was predictable: hearts once tender became hardened, intimacy faded, conversations turned cold, and conflict replaced fellowship. Marriages that could have flourished under God's design became fractured, fragile, or broken.

This book, *When Hearts Grow Hard*, is the natural sequel. It continues the journey, but with a different focus. If the first book was about prevention, this one is about restoration.

Here we examine the root causes of marital drift and breakdown, showing that divorce is rarely the first problem—it is the fruit of hearts that have hardened and turned from God's covenantal design.

It must be stated upfront that this is not a book of blame. It is a book of revelation and hope. God's purpose is never destruction but restoration. His desire is healing, renewal, and covenantal alignment. Even if you entered marriage too quickly, overlooked red flags, or ignored preparation, it is not too late. Hearts can be softened, intimacy can be restored, trust can be rebuilt, and love can be renewed.

This book serves as a roadmap for couples who long to thrive after challenges arise. It will guide you in identifying hardness of heart, restoring emotional and spiritual intimacy, rebuilding trust, forgiving deeply, navigating conflict, resisting external pressures, and in the end rediscovering joy. It is a call to return to God's blueprint, to reclaim covenant love, and to allow your marriage to become a living testimony of His faithfulness.

As Malachi 2:14–15 reminds us, "The Lord was witness between you and the wife of your youth, to whom you have been faithless, though she is your companion and your wife by covenant. Did he not make them one, with a portion of the Spirit in their union? And what was the one God seeking? Godly offspring. So, guard yourselves in your spirit, and let none of you be faithless to the wife of your youth."

Marriage is not merely a human contract but a covenant witnessed by God, designed to reflect His faithfulness. It is a sacred union that must be guarded, nurtured, and aligned with His Spirit.

And as Jesus declared in Mark 10:9, "Therefore what God has joined together, let no one separate."

This is the divine blueprint for marriage—a covenant to be protected, honoured, and lived out as a testimony of God's enduring love.

Introduction

Marriage is one of God's most beautiful gifts, designed not only for companionship but as a living testimony of Christ's covenant love for His Church. Yet in every generation, countless marriages falter—not because love disappears overnight, but because hearts grow hard. Hardness of heart is subtle, often unnoticed until intimacy fades, trust erodes, and distance takes root.

This book was borne out of a burden: to help couples recognise the hidden enemy of hardness, and to rediscover the healing power of forgiveness, tenderness, and covenant love. It is not simply a manual of advice, but a spiritual journey. Each chapter blends biblical truth, practical wisdom, and real-life illustrations to guide husbands and wives back to God's original blueprint for marriage.

You will find here both diagnosis and prescription: why intimacy weakens, how unforgiveness poisons love, and how restoration is always possible through humility, prayer, and grace. Whether your marriage feels strong, strained, or broken, the principles contained inside these pages are meant to equip you, to guard your heart, nurture intimacy, and leave a legacy of covenant faithfulness.

My prayer is that as you read, you will not only gain insight but encounter God's presence. May this book be more than words—it is an invitation to transformation. For when hearts remain soft, marriages flourish. And when marriages flourish, they become sanctuaries of love, unity, and generational strength.

CHAPTER 1

The Scripture That Exposes the Root

"Moses, because of the hardness of your hearts permitted you to divorce your wives: but from the beginning it was not so."
— Matthew 19:8

Marriage is more than a legal contract or social arrangement; it is a divine covenant, ordained by God to mirror His love, unity, and faithfulness. Yet, even the most promising marriages often encounter moments of drift, tension, or despair. While external circumstances—financial stress, infidelity, or miscommunication, can trigger crises; the deeper issue is almost always spiritual and emotional: the condition of the human heart.

Jesus' words in Matthew 19:8 reveal this truth with piercing clarity: divorce is not the root problem. Hardness of heart is.

A Story of Drift

Consider Esther and Daniel. They had been married for ten years. Outwardly, everything appeared normal: they had built a home, achieved career milestones, and raised two children. Friends admired their marriage. Yet beneath the surface, subtle cracks were forming.

One evening, after a long day, Esther approached Daniel:

"I feel like we're just going through the motions, Daniel. We don't really talk anymore," she whispered.

Daniel, exhausted from work, muttered, *"I'm tired, Esther. Can't we talk later?"*

Days turned into weeks. Small slights went unaddressed. Words of affirmation were replaced by silence. Offenses that ordinarily could have been overlooked quietly festered into resentment. Slowly, almost imperceptibly, their hearts began to harden.

By the time they recognised the depth of their emotional distance, the couple felt hopeless. Counselling became necessary not just to fix communication, but to heal hearts that had been hardened over time.

This scenario is not unique to Esther and Daniel. Many marriages begin with love, excitement, and commitment, but small, unresolved offenses, pride, or neglect create slow drift. Jesus calls attention to the heart as the root: fix the heart, and the marriage can be restored; ignore it, and the relationship suffers consequences that are often irreversible.

Understanding Hardness of Heart

The Greek term used in Matthew 19:8 is *sklerokardia*, which means a stubborn, unyielding disposition resistant to God's influence. It is more than emotional hurt; it is a spiritual condition.

A hardened heart:

- Resists forgiveness, even when the offender seeks reconciliation
- Rejects humility, insisting on being right at all costs
- Blocks empathy, making communication cold and mechanical
- Dulls spiritual sensitivity, reducing intimacy with God and spouse

Historically, the Pharisees often sought to manipulate God's law to serve their pride and selfish agendas. Jesus highlighted their condition, demonstrating that obedience without heart alignment is hollow. In marriage, the same principle applies: technical or external fixes—counselling, rules, agreements cannot succeed if the hearts of the spouses remain hardened.

The Spiritual Principle Behind Marital Drift

Jesus' correction, *"from the beginning it was not so"*, points to God's original blueprint for marriage: unity, covenant faithfulness, transparency, and shared dominion. A marriage works best when the hearts of both spouses remain soft, humble, and obedient to God's principles.

When a heart hardens:

- Love becomes conditional
- Communication becomes defensive or manipulative
- Intimacy diminishes
- Spiritual connection weakens
- Conflict escalates quickly

The challenge is that hardness often begins subtly. A lingering offense, unspoken frustration, or quiet resentment can slowly harden the heart. Before couples know it, distance grows, and the once-vibrant bond begins to fade.

Real-Life Illustrations

- The Silent Drift:

John and Grace never fought openly, yet both felt unheard. They avoided conflict at first, thinking silence was safer. Over time, silence became a wedge, and neither realised the depth of emotional erosion until years later.

- The Pride Trap:

A couple refused to apologise after arguments, letting pride dictate behaviour. The inability to admit wrong hardened their hearts, creating a toxic cycle where small disputes escalated into major conflicts.

- The Neglected Heart:

Emily devoted all her energy to her career and children, leaving little attention for her spouse.
Her husband felt unseen, and over time, both hearts hardened from unacknowledged emotional pain.

Each scenario illustrates a critical truth: the heart, not the event, determines the trajectory of a marriage.

- Events are neutral; responses are decisive.

Every marriage faces challenges—financial strain, disagreements, health crises, or unmet expectations. These events are unavoidable. But the way each spouse's heart interprets and reacts to them determines whether the marriage grows stronger or weaker.

- The heart shapes perspective.

A humble, forgiving heart sees conflict as an opportunity for growth. A hardened, prideful heart sees the same conflict as proof of incompatibility. The event is the same; the trajectory diverges because of the heart.

- Spiritual dimension.

In faith-based terms, the heart is the seat of trust in God. Couples who keep their hearts aligned with divine guidance respond to trials with patience, grace, and hope. Those who allow bitterness or selfishness to rule their hearts often drift apart, regardless of the external circumstances.

- Trajectory vs. moment.

A single event doesn't doom or guarantee a marriage. What matters is the cumulative direction of the heart—whether it leans toward love, humility, and reconciliation, or toward resentment, pride, and withdrawal.

Practical Applications: Softening the Heart

To prevent or reverse marital drift, couples must begin by addressing the heart. A daily heart check allows each spouse to reflect on their thoughts, emotions, and attitudes, inviting God to reveal hidden pride, resentment, or selfishness. Confession and humility then become essential, as speaking honestly to God and acknowledging areas of pride, bitterness, or unforgiveness opens the door for His restoration.

Intentional communication is another vital practice. Sharing one honest feeling each day, even when it feels uncomfortable, prevents assumptions and fosters deeper understanding. Prayer for softness strengthens this process, as couples pray individually and together, asking God to soften their hearts, open their ears to one another, and restore trust and intimacy.

Finally, spiritual alignment ensures that the marriage remains rooted in God's design. By spending time together in devotion and worship, couples align their hearts with His blueprint rather than relying on human expectations, allowing covenant love to flourish in strength and unity.

The Truth.

God desires marriages to reflect His covenantal faithfulness. Even when one spouse drifts, a softened heart can ignite restoration. God often moves first in one partner's heart, then orchestrates the reconciliation process.
Small steps in humility and obedience have a domino effect—restoring communication, intimacy, and spiritual alignment.

Reflection Exercises

Reflection begins with honesty. Ask yourself where your heart may have grown hardened—perhaps in areas of communication, trust, or patience—and name three specific places where tenderness has been replaced by resistance. Once those areas are identified, take time to write a letter of forgiveness. You may not share it right away, but the act of putting words on paper will allow grace to do its work and it releases strength which will begin to soften what has been rigid.

From there, cultivate a daily rhythm of gratitude and affirmation toward your spouse. Even small acknowledgments—thanking them for a gesture, affirming their character, or recognising their efforts—can slowly reshape the atmosphere of your marriage. Finally, commit to prayer with intentionality. Each week, ask God for one breakthrough that softens your heart, whether in a particular area of struggle or in your overall posture toward your spouse. Over time, these practices form a pattern of renewal, reminding you that the heart, not the event, sets the trajectory of your relationship.

Prayer

Lord, search my heart. Reveal any areas of pride, bitterness, or unforgiveness. Teach me to love, listen, and forgive quickly. Restore intimacy and unity in my marriage according to Your original design. Soften my heart and the heart of my spouse. May our marriage reflect Your covenantal faithfulness. Amen.

Declaration

"My heart is soft, tender, and receptive to God and my spouse. I release all bitterness, pride, and offense. Love, grace, and unity flow freely in my marriage."

CHAPTER 2

Divorce is the Fruit, Not the Root

"Divorce is not a solution—it is the visible symptom of a deeper problem: the condition of the heart."

Many couples see divorce as the ultimate failure, a catastrophic event that destroys dreams and family structures. Yet, the truth is far deeper: divorce is never the root problem. It is the fruit produced by a hardened heart. Understanding this principle transforms how we approach marriage, conflict, and restoration.

The Story of Mary and Samuel

Mary and Samuel had been married for eight years. Their relationship like many others began with excitement, romance, and shared dreams. But as the years rolled by, little conflicts became regular:
Arguments over finances that were never fully resolved often linger beneath the surface, creating tension that resurfaces in unexpected ways. Silent judgments about career choices can quietly erode trust and respect, leaving one partner feeling unseen or undervalued. Moments of neglect, when love and appreciation went unspoken, may seem small at the time but this gradually build into a sense of distance. Together, these experiences reveal how unaddressed issues and unspoken words can shape the atmosphere of a marriage, not through

the events themselves but through the condition of the heart that responds to them.

Initially, these were minor irritations. Mary assumed Samuel would "understand" her feelings; Samuel assumed Mary was overreacting. Slowly, the emotional distance grew. Walls replaced dialogue. Small offenses were stored in secret, building resentment.

Ten years into their marriage, they reached the breaking point. Divorce papers were signed. Friends were shocked—it "seemed like they had it all together." But the truth was clear: their hearts had hardened long before the divorce happened.

Scriptural Foundation

In Matthew 19:8, Jesus explained:

"Moses, because of the hardness of your hearts permitted you to divorce your wives: but from the beginning it was not so."

Here, Jesus teaches a profound principle: hardness of heart—not sin, circumstance, or disagreement, is the true cause of marital failure. Divorce is simply the external consequence.

What Jesus Reveals

- The Root Is Internal: External problems like arguments, financial struggles, infidelity, become critical only when hearts are hardened. A soft, humble heart can navigate challenges without producing relational death.
- Divorce Is a Symptom: If a marriage ends in divorce, it is usually preceded by years of unnoticed bitterness, pride, and emotional withdrawal.
- God's Original Design: From the beginning, marriage was meant to reflect covenantal love, forgiveness, and unity. Divorce occurs only when the human heart deviates from this divine blueprint.

The Anatomy of Hardness Leading to Divorce

A heart hardens gradually. Understanding this process allows couples to intervene before the “fruit” appears.

Unforgiveness often begins with small offenses that are left unresolved, but over time those unaddressed wounds accumulate and harden into bitterness. Pride adds another layer of division, as the insistence on being right blocks the path to reconciliation and keeps hearts from softening. Neglect, whether emotional, spiritual, or physical, creates a vacuum in the relationship, leaving one or both partners feeling unseen and uncared for. As offenses accumulate—even minor ones—they begin to shape perceptions and emotional reactions, colouring how each spouse interprets the other’s words and actions. Emotional drift follows, as withdrawal and silence gradually replace conversation, eroding intimacy and connection.

Finally, spiritual drift sets in when prayer, worship, and shared devotion fades, leaving the marriage without its deepest source of unity and strength.

Illustration:

Samuel and Mary never realised that their divorce wasn’t caused by a single catastrophic event. It was the culmination of 10 years of quiet emotional erosion—what Jesus calls *hardness of heart*.

Practical Steps to Address the Root

The key to preventing divorce is addressing the root cause: the heart. This begins with a daily heart examination, asking yourself whether resentment, pride, or bitterness have taken root, and journaling honestly while seeking God’s guidance.

It continues with early conflict resolution, refusing to let disagreements fester and choosing instead to speak truth in love, pursuing reconciliation immediately. Intentional forgiveness is also essential, forgiving quickly even when the other party seems undeserving, and releasing bitterness to God so that it does not harden your heart. In addition, Spiritual renewal together strengthens the bond, as couples commit to praying and worshiping daily, studying scripture side by side, and focusing on God's design for marriage.
Finally, counselling and mentorship provide vital support, as godly counsel can prevent problems from escalating, and guidance from a spiritually mature couple offers both insight and accountability. In all of these practices, the condition of the heart remains central, shaping the trajectory of the marriage more than any external circumstance.

The Seed of Restoration:

God often works through one softened heart. Even if one spouse refuses reconciliation, the other's humility, prayer, and obedience can plant seeds of restoration. God honours hearts that seek His will first, creating an atmosphere where broken relationships can revive.

Key Principle: *You cannot control the other heart, but you can govern your own. Softness, obedience, and faithfulness in one heart can shift the destiny of the marriage.*

Reflection Exercises

Begin by identifying the areas in your marriage where unresolved offenses still linger, recognising the places where hurt has not yet been healed. Reflect on the moments when pride or stubbornness stood in the way of reconciliation, and acknowledge how those choices may have created distance. From there, commit to a daily practice of gratitude toward your spouse, offering one small acknowledgment each day that affirms their value and presence in your life.

Finally, dedicate ten minutes in prayer each day, asking God to soften your heart and the heart of your spouse, allowing His grace to restore tenderness and unity where it has been lost.

Prayer:

Lord, I recognise that my heart may be hardened. I surrender pride, resentment, and unforgiveness to You. Teach me to love, to forgive, and to reconcile. Restore the intimacy and unity that reflect Your original design. May my marriage bear the fruit of Your covenant love. Amen.

Declaration:

I release all bitterness, pride, and offense. My heart is tender, my love is active, and my marriage is aligned with God's original plan. Grace, forgiveness, and unity flow in my home.

CHAPTER 3

What Is Hardness of Heart?

"A soft heart receives; a hard heart resists. One nurtures life, the other blocks love."

Marriage flourishes when hearts remain gentle, open, and responsive both to God and to each other. Yet when the heart grows hard, it quietly undermines the relationship from within. It often starts in ways that seem insignificant—minor offenses left unresolved, silent resentments, or prideful thoughts, but if ignored, these seeds of hardness take root. Over time they spread like an invasive vine, choking out love, intimacy, and unity until the bond that once felt strong begins to weaken.

Jesus exposed this in Matthew 19:8 when He said, *"Moses, because of the hardness of your hearts..."*—highlighting the root cause of marital failure.

A Story of Emotional Walls

Consider the marriage of Ruth and James. They had been married for seven years. At first, their love was vibrant, playful, and full of hope. But over time, subtle signs of hardness began to emerge:

- James became quick to anger over minor issues.
- Ruth stopped sharing her feelings, fearing criticism.
- Conversations devolved into defensive statements rather than open dialogue.

One night, Ruth whispered, *"I feel like I'm married to a stranger."*

James, frustrated, muttered, *"Why do you always bring this up?"*

Neither realised that their hearts had silently drifted. Pride had taken root, forgiveness was delayed, and bitterness had quietly grown. By the time they recognised the problem, emotional walls had already formed—walls built from years of unaddressed hardness.

Understanding Hardness of Heart

posture that resists God's love, humility, and reconciliation. This condition reveals itself in many ways. It shows up as a refusal to forgive, where even minor offenses are remembered and carried like weights over time. It appears in defensiveness, when every conversation is treated as a battle to be won rather than a dialogue to be shared. Pride also takes root, driving the desire to be right or to "win," while humility is pushed aside. Emotional withdrawal follows, creating the illusion of safety in distance rather than the risk of genuine connection. Finally, spiritual resistance emerges, as the hardened heart turns away from prayer, counsel, and God's guidance. Together, these patterns form a barrier that suffocates intimacy and obstructs the flow of grace within a marriage. When these traits dominate, even small conflicts escalate into major relational fractures.

The Spiritual Consequence

Hardness of heart does more than wound a marriage—it disrupts the spiritual alignment that sustains it. When resentment, pride, or bitterness are allowed to linger, couples often discover that shared prayer becomes strained or even absent, emotional intimacy begins to fade, decisions shift from collaboration to selfishness, and the flow of God's blessings is delayed or blocked.

Jesus' words in Matthew 19:8 reminds us that obedience to God cannot succeed without the heart being aligned with Him. Counselling sessions, helpful books, and practical strategies may offer guidance, but if the heart remains hardened, the root issue persists.

In time, the fruit of that hardness will inevitably appear in the form of conflict, distance, and even divorce.

Real-Life Illustrations

Hardness of heart rarely arrives suddenly; it grows quietly, almost imperceptibly, through the choices and patterns couples allow to take root. Laura believed she was protecting herself by holding onto minor offenses, but over the years those small grievances accumulated until they formed a wall of resentment. That wall became a barrier to intimacy and trust, leaving her marriage starved of the closeness it once enjoyed. Michael, on the other hand, refused to apologise for his harsh words during arguments. Each unrepented offense hardened his heart and, in turn, his wife's. What began as a single moment of pride became a cycle of defensiveness and coldness, where reconciliation was blocked at every turn. As a way of escape, Laura poured her energy into work and social obligations, unintentionally leaving emotional gaps in her marriage. Her husband, feeling unseen and undervalued, withdrew in response. Over time, both hearts grew distant, and hardness settled in like a quiet frost.

These stories remind us that hardness of heart is not a sudden fracture but a slow erosion. It is shaped by small decisions, unspoken hurts, and emotional neglect. Left unchecked, it becomes a barrier that suffocates love, intimacy, and unity. Yet the very fact that it grows gradually also means it can be reversed gradually—through forgiveness, humility, intentional connection, and a renewed openness to God's guidance.

Practical Steps to Identify and Heal Hardness

A healthy marriage begins with self-examination. Take time to ask yourself whether you are holding onto minor offenses, struggling to forgive quickly, or placing the desire to be right above the call to love your spouse. Honest reflection in these areas opens the door to transformation.

From there, commit to actively softening your heart. Daily prayer for humility and grace creates space for God to reshape your spirit. Journaling helps bring hidden emotions into the light, while deliberate acts of kindness rebuild connection and remind your spouse of their value.

Emotional intimacy must also be nurtured. Set aside uninterrupted time together each week to strengthen your bond. Practice active listening by repeating back what your spouse has shared, showing that you truly understand. Offer affirmations that highlight and reinforce the positive traits you see in one another, cultivating encouragement instead of criticism.

Finally, pursue spiritual alignment as the foundation of your relationship. Pray both together and individually for heart transformation. Study scripture with a focus on God's design for marriage, allowing His Word to guide your union. Seek accountability through mentorship or pastoral counsel, inviting wisdom and support to help you remain steadfast.

Prophetic Insight

God frequently works through softened hearts to bring healing where brokenness has taken root. When even one spouse chooses humility, extends forgiveness, and intentionally seeks reconciliation, the direction of the marriage can be transformed. The Lord takes joy in hearts that embrace obedience and love, rather than clinging to pride or offense.

Key Principle: "I will give you a new heart and put a new spirit in you; I will remove from you your heart of stone and give you a heart of flesh." Ezekiel 36:26

This verse captures the essence of what is described as a soft heart—what Ezekiel calls a "heart of flesh." This is an open, tender, and receptive heart to God's presence. It becomes the place where His Spirit can dwell, releasing grace, intimacy, and power into the marriage. By contrast, a hardened heart, or "heart of stone," resists that divine influence, creating distance not only between spouses but also between the couple and God.

In the context of marriage, this scripture reminds us that transformation begins with the heart. When one or both spouses allow God to replace hardness with tenderness, reconciliation and renewal become possible. The marriage then shifts from being shaped by pride, resentment, or bitterness to being sustained by humility, forgiveness, and love.

Closing Prayer

Lord, search my heart. Remove every trace of hardness, pride, and resentment. Teach me to forgive quickly, love intentionally, and pursue unity with my spouse. Let our hearts reflect Your covenantal design. Amen.

Declaration

"My heart is soft and tender. I release all bitterness, pride, and offense. Grace, unity, and love flow freely in my marriage. Our hearts are aligned with God's will and covenant."

CHAPTER 4

The Slow Death Before the Final Blow

"Marriage does not collapse in a single moment; it dies slowly, silently, spiritually."

Divorce or marital breakdown is rarely sudden. Like a tree slowly dying from within, the roots of a marriage can decay long before the branches fall apart. Understanding the stages of decline allows couples to make early intervention, heal their hearts, and restore unity before it is too late.

Jesus' words in Matthew 19:8 emphasise the heart as the root cause of marital failure. This chapter will explore the subtle, progressive stages of decline, showing how a marriage can drift from intimacy to emotional and spiritual detachment.

A Story of Gradual Drift

Hannah and Peter entered marriage full of excitement and shared dreams, but over time the pressures of life began to reshape their relationship. Disappointment surfaced first, as Hannah longed for expressions of love that Peter did not naturally offer, leaving him feeling criticised and unappreciated. Hurt then began to accumulate, with small, slight and unresolved arguments quietly festering beneath the surface. Gradually, withdrawal took hold; they stopped sharing their feelings and thoughts, speaking only when necessary. Silence soon became the norm, reducing their conversations to functional exchanges rather than moments of intimacy. Bitterness seeped in, colouring their perceptions and turning minor issues into major irritations.

Coldness followed, as physical affection, emotional warmth, and words of encouragement faded away. Eventually, detachment set in, and though they lived under the same roof, they inhabited emotionally in separate worlds.

By the time they recognised the depth of the problem, reconciliation demanded more than casual effort, it required spiritual guidance, intentional heart work, and a renewed commitment to rebuild what had quietly eroded.

The Slow Drift of Marital Decline

Marriages rarely collapse overnight. Instead, they unravel gradually, often through a series of subtle stages that erode trust, intimacy, and unity. The first stage is disappointment. Expectations—sometimes unspoken, go unmet, and misunderstandings plant seeds of dissatisfaction. What begins as a small gap between desire and reality can quietly grow into discontent if left unacknowledged.

Hurt follows close behind. Emotional wounds that are not addressed begin to accumulate. Even minor offenses, when carried over time, gain weight and create resentment.

This is the moment where couples can intervene—by naming the hurt, seeking forgiveness, and choosing reconciliation before bitterness takes root.

When hurt is ignored, withdrawal often sets in. Instead of expressing pain, spouses retreat emotionally. Conversations lose depth, intimacy diminishes, and the relationship begins to feel more functional than personal. Silence then becomes the norm. Without communication, assumptions and misinterpretations thrive, widening the emotional distance.

Here again lies a turning point: couples who choose to break the silence and re-engage in honest dialogue can prevent the drift from deepening.

Bitterness emerges as accumulated offenses harden the heart. Perceptions shift, and even minor conflicts feel insurmountable. Coldness follows, stripping away emotional warmth, spiritual closeness, and physical affection. The marriage that once thrived on encouragement and tenderness now feels barren and drained of energy. At this stage, intentional acts of kindness, humility, and forgiveness can begin to thaw the frost if both partners are willing.

Detachment is the penultimate stage. Partners live parallel lives, sharing space but not joy, vision, or spiritual engagement. The final rupture—divorce or separation, becomes the visible outcome, the fruit of years of neglected hearts and unresolved pain. Yet even here, intervention is possible. With humility, spiritual renewal, and a commitment to heart work, couples can rebuild what has been lost.

The Turning Points

What makes this progression so sobering is also what makes it hopeful: at nearly every stage, there is an opportunity to intervene. Disappointment can be met with honest conversation. Hurt can be healed through forgiveness. Withdrawal can be reversed by choosing vulnerability. Silence can be broken with intentional dialogue. Bitterness can be softened through humility. Coldness can be warmed by deliberate acts of love. Detachment can be challenged by re-engaging in shared vision and spiritual alignment.

Marital decline is not inevitable. It is the result of choices—some small, some significant—that accumulate over time. But just as decline is gradual, so too is restoration. Couples who choose to soften their hearts, seek reconciliation, and invite God's guidance can reverse the trajectory, rediscovering intimacy and unity where distance once prevailed.

Scriptural Perspective

Hardness of heart is more than an emotional problem; it is spiritual. The Bible consistently emphasises the heart as the seat of life and relationship:

- *"Keep your heart with all vigilance, for from it flow the springs of life"* (Proverbs 4:23).
- *"A glad heart makes a cheerful face, but by sorrow of the heart, the spirit is broken"* (Proverbs 15:13).

Jesus' observation in Matthew 19:8 reminds us that the condition of the heart shapes every relational outcome.
If the heart hardens, even minor disagreements escalate, and the marriage drifts toward the slow death described above.

Practical Steps for Early Intervention

The good news is that recognising these stages of decline makes it possible to take corrective action before the damage becomes irreversible. It begins with noticing the early signs—emotional withdrawal, avoidance of conversation, or a decrease in affection. Once these patterns are identified, hurt must be addressed immediately through confession and forgiveness so that resentment does not have the chance to accumulate. Communication should be maintained intentionally, with weekly check-ins that create space for sharing feelings and concerns openly.

Couples can then reignite emotional connection by planning moments of joy, fun, and shared experiences that remind them of their bond. Spiritual intimacy is equally vital, nurtured through daily prayer, studying scripture together, and worshiping as a couple. Finally, mentorship and counselling provide guidance and accountability, offering the wisdom of spiritually mature couples or pastoral support before problems escalate. When these practices are embraced, the trajectory of the marriage can shift from decline toward renewal and strength.

Illustrations of Early Intervention

Marital decline often begins quietly, but couples who act early can change the story. Anna and Mark noticed the signs of withdrawal before it became entrenched. Rather than ignoring the distance, they committed to a weekly "heart check" conversation. In those moments, they shared disappointments honestly, practiced forgiveness, and carved out intentional time together. Over the course of months, the cracks that had begun to form healed, preventing them from widening into fractures. Their choice to intervene early transformed what could have become bitterness into renewed closeness.

Rebekah and John's journey was more advanced. By the time they sought help, bitterness had already taken root. Yet instead of allowing it to harden further, they turned to mentorship with a seasoned couple. Through prayer, guidance, and practical exercises, they learned to soften their hearts again. Emotional intimacy, which had been buried under layers of resentment, began to return. Their story shows that even when decline has progressed, outside wisdom and accountability can provide the tools for restoration.

In a seemingly more complex situation, Sarah and Daniel had drifted into coldness, their marriage dulled by years of gradual detachment. Waking up from their sudden slumber, they chose prayer as their catalyst for change, setting aside thirty minutes each evening to pray together and share one positive affirmation daily. This rhythm of spiritual connection reignited warmth between them, reversing the distance that had quietly taken hold. What seemed like a settled state of emotional separation was undone by consistent, intentional practices that reawakened their bond.

The Common Thread

These stories highlight a crucial truth: decline is not inevitable. Whether couples intervene at the first signs of withdrawal, in the midst of bitterness, or even after coldness has set in, deliberate action can redirect the trajectory of the marriage. Small, intentional steps—conversation, mentorship, prayer—become turning points that prevent fractures from becoming permanent. The earlier the intervention, the easier the restoration, but even late efforts can breathe life back into a relationship when hearts are willing to soften.

Prophetic Insight

God is always at work in the hidden places of the heart. Even when a marriage feels as though it is slipping into slow decline, the willingness of just one spouse to soften, to humble themselves, and to pursue reconciliation can open the door to divine restoration. Early obedience—acknowledging pride or resentment with humility—draws God's intervention. Active love, expressed through deliberate acts of kindness, interrupts the cycle of withdrawal and begins to rebuild connection. Spiritual focus, through prayer and worship, restores covenant alignment and re-centres the marriage on God's design.

The key principle is clear: marriages falter when hearts drift spiritually, emotionally, and relationally. Yet restoration begins the very moment one heart chooses obedience, humility, and intentional love. From that choice, God's presence is invited back into the union, and what seemed broken beyond repair can be renewed.

Reflection Exercises

Begin by reviewing your marriage with honesty, asking yourself which stage your relationship may currently be in.

Take time to recognise the small offenses or disappointments you may have been holding onto, and bring them into the light rather than allowing them to accumulate. Commit to one act of emotional connection each day this week—something simple yet intentional that reminds your spouse of your love. Finally, set aside time for a weekly "heart-to-heart," a conversation devoted not to logistics or tasks but to sharing feelings, listening deeply, and strengthening your bond.

Prayer

Lord, reveal any subtle hardness in my heart and in the heart of my spouse. Teach us to forgive quickly, to communicate openly, and to restore both emotional and spiritual intimacy. Reverse every stage of drift and align our hearts with Your covenant plan. Amen.

Declaration

I choose obedience, humility, and love. I reject bitterness, pride, and withdrawal. My marriage is restored in heart, spirit, and intimacy. Grace and unity flow continuously in our home.

CHAPTER 5

"From the Beginning It Was Not So" — God's Original Blueprint

"But from the beginning it was not so."
— Matthew 19:8

Marriage is not a human invention or a subject of social convenience, it is God's divine institution, designed to reflect His love, covenant, and purpose. Yet, when couples drift apart or their hearts get hardened, they lose sight of the original blueprint, creating space for conflict, misunderstanding, and even divorce.

This chapter explores God's original design, showing how couples can restore unity, love, and covenantal alignment by returning to His principles.

A Story of Rediscovery

Take the story of Samuel and Lydia. Married for twelve years, they had weathered numerous storms: career pressures, parenting struggles, and financial strain. Over time, subtle hardening of hearts led to emotional distance.

One evening, during a rare moment of honest conversation, Samuel blurted out:

"Lydia, I feel like we've lost sight of what God intended for us."

Lydia replied quietly: *"I've been feeling the same, Samuel. Maybe we need to go back to the beginning—remember why we married, and what God's heart for marriage really is."*

That conversation marked the beginning of their restoration. They committed to rediscover God's blueprint, rebuilding their relationship on His original design rather than human expectations or cultural norms.

God's Original Design for Marriage

When Jesus declared, "from the beginning it was not so", He reminded us that divorce and marital drift were never part of God's plan. From creation, marriage was intended to be a covenant of unity—a bond that joins two hearts, minds, and spirits into one. As Genesis 2:24 affirms, "Therefore, a man shall leave his father and mother and hold fast to his wife, and they shall become one flesh." This unity requires humility, communication, and a shared purpose. It also echoes the principle found in Amos 3:3: "Do two walk together unless they have agreed to do so?" True unity in marriage depends on agreement—walking in the same direction spiritually, emotionally, and relationally.

Marriage was also designed as a relationship of transparency. God desires honesty and openness between spouses, knowing that hidden resentment, secrets, or unspoken expectations erode trust and intimacy. Alongside transparency comes shared dominion and partnership. Marriage reflects God's collaborative design, where stewardship of life and household flows from mutual respect and a shared vision. Decisions and responsibilities are not meant to be carried out alone but embraced together in unity.

Mutual respect and honour form the soil in which love flourishes. As Ephesians 5:33 teaches, "However, let each one of you love his wife as himself, and let the wife see that she respects her husband." Respect nurtures love, ensuring that both spouses feel valued and cherished.

God's design also calls couples into fellowship and spiritual alignment. Prayer, worship, and seeking

His guidance together strengthen not only spiritual connection but also emotional and physical intimacy. A marriage rooted in shared pursuit of God becomes resilient against drift.

Finally, harmony in conflict is part of God's blueprint. Marriage was never meant to be free of disagreements, but rather it is designed to be a place where differences are navigated with love, patience, and forgiveness. Conflict, when handled with grace, becomes an opportunity for growth rather than division.

God's Blueprint vs. Human Deviation

From the beginning, God designed marriage to be a covenant of unity, transparency, respect, and spiritual alignment. Genesis 2:24 declares, "Therefore a man shall leave his father and mother and hold fast to his wife, and they shall become one flesh." This unity is not merely physical but emotional and spiritual, requiring humility, communication, and shared purpose. Amos 3:3 reinforces this truth: "Do two walk together unless they have agreed to do so?" Agreement and alignment are essential for a marriage to flourish.

Yet when couples deviate from this blueprint, the drift begins. Emotional distance develops as hearts grow guarded, and communication deteriorates when honesty and gentleness are replaced with silence or harsh words. Proverbs 15:1 reminds us, "A gentle answer turns away wrath, but a harsh word stirs up anger." Without gentleness, pride and offense take root, blocking reconciliation. James 4:6 warns, "God opposes the proud but shows favour to the humble." Pride hardens the heart, while humility invites grace.

God's design also calls for transparency and mutual respect. Ephesians 5:33 teaches, "Let each one of you love his wife as himself, and let the wife see that she respects her husband." Respect is the soil in which love flourishes.

But when hidden resentment, secrets, or neglect replace openness, intimacy erodes. Spiritual drift follows, as prayer and worship diminish, leaving couples walking in different directions.

Ultimately, deviation from God's plan leads to rupture. Jesus explained in Matthew 19:8, "Moses permitted you to divorce your wives because your hearts were hard. But it was not this way from the beginning." Divorce or relational collapse is not the fruit of God's design but of hardened hearts and neglected covenant.

The Contrast

- God's Design: Unity, transparency, respect, shared purpose, spiritual alignment, and harmony in conflict.
- Human Deviation: Emotional distance, broken communication, pride, spiritual drift, bitterness, and eventual rupture.

Every broken pattern in marriage can be traced back to deviation from God's original plan. Yet the hope remains: restoration begins the moment one heart chooses obedience, humility, and intentional love. When couples return to God's blueprint, His presence restores intimacy, grace, and covenant strength.

Practical Steps to Restore God's Blueprint

Restoring God's design for marriage begins with the heart. Realignment requires confession of pride, bitterness, and offense, followed by a sincere request for God to renew tenderness and commitment. As Psalm 51:10 prays, "Create in me a clean heart, O God, and renew a right spirit within me." When hearts are softened, reconciliation becomes possible.

From there, couples must rediscover unity. Intentional quality time, shared goals, and daily reflections rebuild the bond that Genesis 2:24 describes: "Therefore a man shall leave his father and mother and hold fast to his wife, and they shall become one flesh." Unity is not accidental; it is cultivated through deliberate togetherness.

Transparency is equally vital. Honest sharing of feelings, struggles, and hopes prevents hidden resentment from eroding intimacy. Proverbs 24:26 reminds us, "An honest answer is like a kiss on the lips." Emotional honesty is a gift that deepens trust and connection.

Partnership reflects God's collaborative design. Dividing responsibilities fairly, consulting one another in major decisions, and celebrating each other's contributions embody

Ecclesiastes 4:9–10: "Two are better than one, because they have a good return for their labour: if either of them falls down, one can help the other up." Marriage thrives when both spouses carry the load together.

Respect and honour form the soil in which love flourishes. Daily affirmations, valuing each other's opinions, and acknowledging one another both publicly and privately fulfil Ephesians 5:33: "Let each one of you love his wife as himself, and let the wife see that she respects her husband."

Finally, spiritual connection strengthens every other dimension of marriage. Couples who pray, worship, and study God's Word together invite His presence into their union. Matthew 18:20 assures us, "For where two or three are gathered in my name, there am I among them." Spiritual intimacy fortifies emotional and physical closeness, aligning the marriage with God's covenant plan.

This framework shows that restoration is not abstract—it is practical, intentional, and deeply rooted in scripture. Each step counters the drift of neglect and reestablishes the foundation God intended from the beginning.

Illustrative Examples

Thomas and Naomi's marriage had grown cold, marked by distance and fading affection. Recognising the drift, they chose to begin weekly devotional nights, sharing personal prayer requests and recommitting themselves to God's design for marriage. Over time, these intentional practices rekindled intimacy and joy, proving that even coldness can be reversed when hearts turn back to God and to each other.

Elijah and Ruth faced constant tension in decision-making, often clashing over household responsibilities and spiritual direction. Their breakthrough came when they embraced true partnership, intentionally consulting one another and sharing both practical and spiritual responsibilities. This shift brought harmony, mutual respect, and a renewed sense of shared spiritual authority, reflecting the biblical principle of "two are better than one" (Ecclesiastes 4:9).

Mary and Peter realised that their growing distance was rooted in neglecting God's covenant. They chose to return to spiritual alignment by praying together daily, reading scripture, and engaging in honest conversations about their struggles and hopes. As their hearts softened, love and unity were renewed, embodying the truth of Amos 3:3: "Do two walk together unless they have agreed to do so?" Their agreement to walk together spiritually restored the foundation of their marriage.

These examples highlight that restoration is possible at every stage of decline. Whether through devotion, partnership, or spiritual realignment, couples who choose obedience, humility, and intentional love can reverse drift and rediscover the joy of covenant marriage.

Prophetic Insight

God's blueprint for marriage is eternal and unchanging. It is not subject to culture, convenience, or circumstance.

When couples choose obedience, humility, and covenantal love, their union becomes a living conduit of God’s grace, blessing, and favour. A soft heart aligned with Him restores emotional intimacy, breaking down walls of distance and resentment. Spiritual partnership activates divine guidance, ensuring that decisions and directions are shaped by His wisdom rather than human pride. Unity in purpose brings resilience, enabling couples to navigate life’s trials with strength and hope.

The key principle is this: returning to God’s original design for marriage is not a mere task to be checked off—it is a transformative journey. It is the process of restoring love, intimacy, and covenantal alignment, step by step, as hearts yield to His Spirit.

Reflection Exercises

Take time to prayerfully examine your marriage. Begin by listing the ways your relationship may currently deviate from God’s original design—whether through emotional distance, lack of transparency, or neglect of spiritual practices. Then, identify three practical steps you can take to restore unity, transparency, and respect.

These may be as simple as speaking affirmations daily, setting aside time for honest conversation, or sharing responsibilities in fairness.

Commit together to pray daily for one month, focusing specifically on heart alignment and covenant restoration. Let prayer become the anchor that draws your hearts back into God’s presence. Finally, write down shared dreams or goals, ensuring they align with His blueprint. As Amos 3:3 reminds us, “Do two walk together unless they have agreed to do so?” Agreement in vision and purpose is essential for covenant strength.

This structure not only calls couples to reflection but also provides a pathway for renewal, showing how obedience and intentional love can restore what drift has eroded.

Prayer

Lord, restore my marriage to Your original design. Heal hearts, renew intimacy, and align our spirits with Your covenant plan. Let love, unity, respect, and shared purpose flourish. Teach us to navigate conflict with humility and grace, reflecting Your glory in our relationship. Amen.

Declaration

My marriage is restored to God's original design. Our hearts are tender, our spirits aligned, and our covenant renewed. Love, grace, and unity flow continuously in our home.

CHAPTER 6

The Spiritual Battle Behind Hardness of Heart

"For we do not wrestle against flesh and blood, but against principalities, against powers, against the rulers of the darkness of this age, against spiritual hosts of wickedness in the heavenly places."
— Ephesians 6:12

Marriage is not only a relational covenant but also a spiritual battlefield. What appears as ordinary conflict—disagreements, pride, resentment, or emotional withdrawal—is often a symptom of a deeper, spiritual struggle. When couples fail to recognise this, they can fight each other while the real enemy works silently, strengthening hardness of heart and weakening unity.

A Story of Unseen Battles

Consider Daniel and Abigail. Married for nine years, everything about the appeared quite normal on the outside: stable careers, happy children, a well-kept home. Yet, the couple constantly argued over small things: finances, household responsibilities, time management.

One night, Daniel said in frustration, *"I don't understand why you're so difficult!"*

Abigail responded bitterly, *"And I don't understand why you never listen!"*

What they did not recognise was that they were fighting symptoms, not the root cause.

Years of unaddressed emotional offenses, combined with spiritual attacks targeting their unity, had hardened their hearts. Each argument strengthened walls of pride, resentment, and bitterness—tools the enemy uses to weaken God's covenant.

Understanding the Spiritual Dimension

Jesus taught that the heart is the true battlefield. Hardness of heart is not merely psychological—it is deeply spiritual. When unforgiveness lingers, it opens the door to bitterness, resentment, and even spiritual oppression. Pride and selfishness then take root, keeping couples from reconciliation and unity. Emotional neglect weakens the spiritual bond, leaving hearts vulnerable to external influences. Unresolved offenses, left to fester, sow seed of conflict and emotional distance, often exploited by spiritual forces, and this seek to divide what God has joined together.

The Apostle Paul reminds us in Ephesians 6:12: "For we wrestle not against flesh and blood, but against principalities, against powers, against the rulers of the darkness of this world, against spiritual wickedness in high places." This truth reframes marital conflict. The real battle is not against one's spouse but against spiritual forces that aim to derail God's covenant plan. Recognising this infiltration shifts the posture of the heart: conflict is no longer about winning an argument but about preserving unity, covenant, and spiritual alignment.

When couples understand the spiritual dimension, they begin to fight differently. Forgiveness becomes a weapon against bitterness. Humility disarms pride. Emotional attentiveness strengthens spiritual connection. And reconciliation closes the door to the enemy's schemes. In this way, the marriage becomes not just a relationship but a testimony of God's power to overcome division and restore covenant love.

The Enemy's Strategy in Marriage

Marriage is a covenant designed by God, but the enemy seeks to undermine it through subtle strategies. Isolation weakens communication, creating emotional distance where intimacy once thrived. Distraction overloads couples with work, social commitments, and life pressures, diverting attention from spiritual intimacy. Resentment amplification takes past offenses and magnifies them, fuelling current arguments and deepening division. Finally, spiritual discouragement whispers hopelessness, convincing couples that reconciliation is impossible and leaving them feeling trapped.

Ephesians 6:12 reminds us, "For we wrestle not against flesh and blood, but against principalities, against powers, against the rulers of the darkness of this world, against spiritual wickedness in high places." The true battle is not against one's spouse but against spiritual forces that aim to derail God's covenant plan. Recognising this shifts the perspective: conflict is not about winning but about preserving unity, covenant, and spiritual alignment.

Practical Spiritual Warfare Strategies

To counteract these forces, couples must engage both practically and spiritually. Guarding the heart is the first defence. Daily prayer for protection over one's own heart and the heart of one's spouse builds a shield against bitterness and hardness. Speaking scripture over the marriage, such as Isaiah 54:17— "No weapon formed against our union shall prosper"—anchors the relationship in God's promises.

Cultivating forgiveness is essential. Offenses must be released to God immediately, before resentment takes root. Confessing bitterness or pride to Him and to each other disarms the enemy's schemes and restores tenderness.

Strengthening spiritual connection is another vital strategy. Couples who pray and worship together daily, and who study God's Word with a focus on covenantal promises, invite His presence into their union. Matthew 18:20 assures us, "For where two or three are gathered in my name, there am I among them."

Recognising patterns early prevents small cracks from becoming fractures. Emotional withdrawal, coldness, or repeated arguments should be seen as spiritual red flags. Addressing these issues promptly, with humility and love, closes the door to division.

Finally, declaring God's covenant over the marriage is a powerful act of spiritual warfare. Speaking life and unity daily reinforces the truth of God's design. Declarations such as, "Our hearts are united in love and covenant. Hardness and division have no place in our home," establish faith-filled agreement and remind both spouses of their shared commitment.

Key Principle

The enemy's strategy is subtle but predictable. God's strategy, however, is eternal and victorious. When couples guard their hearts, cultivate forgiveness, strengthen spiritual connection, recognise patterns early, and declare covenant truth, they not only resist the enemy's schemes but actively restore the beauty of God's original design for marriage.

Illustrations of Spiritual Warfare in Marriage

Rebecca and Paul found themselves locked in constant arguments over small misunderstandings. What seemed trivial grew into walls of bitterness that separated their hearts. Yet when they chose to pray together, asking God to expose hidden pride and unforgiveness, something shifted. Emotional barriers softened, and relational clarity returned.

Their story reflects James 5:16: "Therefore confess your sins to each other and pray for each other so that you may be healed." Prayer became the weapon that dismantled bitterness and restored peace.

Lisa and Jonathan endured repeated marital strain, unable to break free from cycles of unresolved offenses. Through consistent fasting, prayer, and meditation on scripture, they discerned that spiritual attacks were fuelling their conflicts. By addressing these battles spiritually, they transformed their interactions and rediscovered unity. Their obedience echoes Matthew 17:21, where Jesus taught that certain breakthroughs come only "by prayer and fasting." Their willingness to fight spiritually brought divine intervention into their marriage.

Mary and Peter's journey illustrates the power of one heart. Even when one spouse resists reconciliation, a single obedient, prayerful heart can activate restoration. God honours the willing partner, breaking chains of hardness and opening doors for healing. This truth reflects 1 Corinthians 7:14, which teaches that the believing spouse sanctifies the union, allowing God's grace to flow even when faith is unevenly shared. One heart yielded to God can shift the atmosphere of an entire marriage.

These examples remind us that spiritual warfare in marriage is real, but so is God's power to restore. Bitterness can be dismantled through prayer, spiritual attacks can be overcome through obedience, and even one softened heart can invite divine restoration.

Prophetic Insight

Hardness of heart is both a symptom and a battlefield. It reveals where pride, anger, or unforgiveness have taken root, and it becomes the ground upon which spiritual warfare is fought.

God, in His wisdom, often allows adversity, conflict, and resistance to bring to the surface these hidden issues—not to destroy, but to expose what must be surrendered. As Proverbs 4:23 reminds us, "Above all else, guard your heart, for everything you do flows from it."

When couples respond to these challenges with humility, prayer, and love, the hardness begins to break. Forgiveness softens what pride has hardened, prayer invites God's presence into the struggle, and love restores what offense has fractured. In this posture of obedience, God not only heals relationships but also releases spiritual blessings. As James 4:6 declares, "God opposes the proud but shows favour to the humble." Favour flows where humility reigns.

The battlefield of the heart, then, is not a place of defeat but of transformation. What the enemy intends for division, God uses as an opportunity for renewal. When couples yield to His Spirit, He turns conflict into clarity, adversity into growth, and resistance into resilience. The result is not merely restored intimacy but a marriage that becomes a conduit of grace, blessing, and covenant strength.

Key Principle: *Marriage is victorious when couples fight the spiritual battle together, guard their hearts, and allow God to remove every trace of hardness, pride, and resentment.*

Reflection Exercises

Begin by praying for revelation, asking the Lord to uncover where spiritual influences may have contributed to hardness in your marriage. Allow Him to bring hidden pride, unforgiveness, or neglect into the open so that healing can begin.

Next, identify one unresolved offense that you have carried in your heart.

Release it in prayer, surrendering it fully to God and choosing forgiveness over bitterness. This act of release opens the door for reconciliation and renewed tenderness.

Commit with your spouse to a daily covenant prayer. Even a few minutes of united prayer each day strengthens spiritual alignment and invites God's presence into your relationship. As Matthew 18:20 assures us, "For where two or three are gathered in my name, there am I among them."

Finally, keep a record of moments where emotional drift appears—instances of withdrawal, silence, or distance. Pray specifically over each one, asking God to restore intimacy and unity. By naming these areas and lifting them before Him, you close the door to division and invite His Spirit to rebuild what has been weakened.

Prayer

Lord, we acknowledge the spiritual battles surrounding our marriage. Reveal any hardness, pride, or unforgiveness in our hearts. Teach us to fight together, not against each other, and to allow Your love, unity, and covenant to prevail. Amen.

Declaration

Our marriage is fortified against spiritual attack. Hardness, bitterness, and division have no place in our home. We walk in unity, love, and God's covenantal favour.

CHAPTER 7

Identifying the Drift Before It Becomes Permanent

"The heart of a fool is in his mouth, but the mouth of the wise brings healing."
— Proverbs 12:18

Marriages rarely fail overnight. Most marriages begin to drift quietly, imperceptibly, until emotional, spiritual, and relational distance has set in. The key to saving a marriage is recognising the early warning signs of drift—before they harden into walls that separate hearts permanently.

Jesus' teaching in Matthew 19:8 reminds us that the heart is the root of all relational outcomes. If a heart drifts, the marriage drifts. If a heart softens, the marriage thrives.

A Story of Early Warning Signs

Naomi and David began their marriage full of love, joy, and hope for the future. In the early days, their connection felt effortless. Yet, as time passed, subtle shifts began to creep in. Naomi noticed that David seemed increasingly distracted during their conversations, his attention pulled elsewhere. David, on the other hand, began to interpret Naomi's emotional responses as "overreactions," dismissing her feelings rather than engaging with them. Instead of asking clarifying questions, both started making assumptions about each other's intentions.

What began as small irritations went unaddressed. minor disagreements, were left unresolved, slowly they escalated into larger arguments.

Without realising it, Naomi and David drifted into emotional disconnection.

The warmth and openness that once defined their relationship gave way to distance and misunderstanding.

This story illustrates a sobering truth: early drift in marriage is often silent, gradual, and easily ignored. It rarely announces itself with dramatic conflict at first; instead, it hides in distraction, assumptions, and unspoken hurts. Yet, the good news is that such drift is reversible if caught in time. When couples choose to notice the warning signs, address them with humility, and re-engage in honest communication, the trajectory can shift back toward intimacy and unity.

Recognising Early Signs of Drift

Marital drift seldom announces itself through explosive conflict. Instead, it often creeps in quietly, through small, almost imperceptible changes that gradually erode closeness. Intimacy weakens not in a single moment, but through overlooked patterns of distance and silence. The key to restoration lies in noticing these subtle signals early, before they harden into disconnection, and choosing to address them with humility and intentional love.

Emotional withdrawal is often the first indicator. One or both spouses begin to avoid meaningful conversation, and intimacy declines as dreams, fears, and daily experiences are no longer shared. Proverbs 18:1 warns, “Whoever isolates himself seeks his own desire; he breaks out against all sound judgment.” Withdrawal creates space and breeds division.

Increased criticism follows. Small mistakes or habits become major points of contention, and words shift from constructive to harsh or dismissive. Proverbs 15:1 reminds us, “A gentle answer turns away wrath, but a harsh word stirs up anger.” Criticism erodes trust and breeds defensiveness.

Loss of shared vision is another sign. Couples stop discussing goals, plans, or spiritual alignment, and individual priorities overshadow the shared purpose of marriage. Amos 3:3 asks, "Do two walk together unless they have agreed to do so?" Without agreement, unity falters.

Physical and emotional coldness emerges as affection, warmth, and encouragement decrease. Silence or distance replaces loving touch and comforting words. Song of Solomon 2:15 cautions, "Catch the foxes for us, the little foxes that spoil the vineyards." Small neglects can spoil intimacy if left unchecked.

Frequent misunderstandings take root when simple statements are misinterpreted as attacks. Defensiveness and pride prevent open communication. James 1:19 offers wisdom: "Let every person be quick to hear, slow to speak, slow to anger." Listening with humility prevents misinterpretation.

Neglecting spiritual connection is perhaps the most dangerous drift. Prayer, worship, and study together become rare, and spiritual alignment weakens under daily pressures. Matthew 18:20 assures us, "For where two or three are gathered in my name, there am I among them." Without shared pursuit of God, marriages lose their anchor.

Finally, persistent bitterness or resentment festers when past offenses are remembered repeatedly and forgiveness is delayed. Hebrews 12:15 warns, "See to it that no root of bitterness springs up and causes trouble, and by it many become defiled." Bitterness poisons intimacy and blocks restoration.

Key Principle

Early drift is silent, gradual, and often ignored—but it is reversible if caught in time. By recognising these warning signs and responding with humility, forgiveness, and spiritual alignment, couples can close the door to division and restore the covenant strength God intended.

The Consequence of Ignoring Early Drift

When early signs of marital drift are ignored, they gradually harden the heart—the very condition Jesus warned against in Matthew 19:8: "Moses permitted you to divorce your wives because your hearts were hard.

But it was not this way from the beginning." What begins as subtle distance eventually creates emotional walls that separate spouses. Trust and intimacy erode, leaving the relationship vulnerable to misunderstanding and resentment.

Conflict then intensifies. Small disagreements escalate into battles, and unresolved offenses become fuel for division. As intimacy weakens, the marriage becomes increasingly susceptible to spiritual attack, echoing the warning of Ephesians 6:12: "For we wrestle not against flesh and blood, but against principalities, against powers…" The enemy exploits drift, magnifying bitterness and discouragement.

Left unchecked, these patterns set the stage for divorce or permanent separation. What God designed as a covenant of unity becomes fractured by neglect and hardness of heart.

This is why early intervention is critical. Once hearts harden, reconciliation requires far greater effort, deeper prayer, and often a spiritual breakthrough. Yet the hope remains: when couples choose humility, forgiveness, and intentional love, God can soften even the hardest heart and restore what seemed beyond repair.

Key Principle

Every consequence of drift has a spiritual antidote. Emotional distance is healed by intentional connection, mistrust by transparency, conflict by gentleness, vulnerability by prayer, and separation by covenantal commitment. When couples apply these counter-strategies, they not only resist the enemy's schemes but actively restore God's original design for marriage.

Practical Steps to Counter Early Drift

Daily Heart Check

Ask yourself honestly: Am I withdrawing, judging, or holding offense? Confess any pride, bitterness, or resentment to God and, when needed, to your spouse.

Scripture Anchor: "Search me, O God, and know my heart; test me and know my anxious thoughts." (Psalm 139:23)

Intentional Communication

Set aside time each day for meaningful conversation—beyond logistics and schedules. Avoid assumptions; instead, ask clarifying questions to understand feelings and intentions.

Scripture Anchor: "Let every person be quick to hear, slow to speak, slow to anger." (James 1:19)

Emotional Reconnection

Engage in shared activities that spark joy and strengthen your bond. Express appreciation and love intentionally through words, gestures, and encouragement.

Scripture Anchor: "Encourage one another and build each other up." (1 Thessalonians 5:11)

Reestablish Shared Vision

Discuss both short-term and long-term goals together. Align priorities, values, and spiritual direction as a couple, ensuring unity of purpose.

Scripture Anchor: “Do two walk together unless they have agreed to do so?” (Amos 3:3)

Strengthen Spiritual Partnership

Pray together daily, read scripture, and worship as a couple. Use spiritual disciplines—fasting, declarations, and thanksgiving—to guard your hearts and home.

Scripture Anchor: “For where two or three are gathered in my name, there am I among them.” (Matthew 18:20)

Key Principle

Early drift is reversible when couples choose humility, intentionality, and spiritual alignment. These practices are not just habits—they are weapons of spiritual warfare that protect intimacy, restore unity, and reinforce covenant love.

Illustrations of Early Intervention

The Saved Marriage

Grace and Michael began to notice subtle withdrawal in their relationship—conversations grew shorter, and appreciation was less frequent. Rather than ignoring these signs, they chose early intervention. Weekly heart check-ins gave them space to share openly, daily prayer re-centred their covenant in God’s presence, and intentional words of appreciation rekindled warmth. Their proactive steps reversed drift before hardening occurred, embodying Hebrews 3:13: “Encourage one another daily… so that none of you may be hardened by sin’s deceitfulness.”

Spiritual Alignment as a Shield

Hannah and Peter recognised that emotional coldness was leaving them vulnerable to conflict. Instead of allowing distance to grow, they committed to daily devotionals and prayer together. This spiritual discipline softened their hearts, renewed unity, and shielded them from the enemy's schemes. Their story reflects Ecclesiastes 4:12: "A cord of three strands is not quickly broken." By inviting God into their union, they discovered resilience against division.

The Power of Proactive Love

Sometimes the most effective interventions are simple. Small, intentional acts of love—texts of encouragement, spoken affirmations, shared meals—can prevent drift from becoming permanent. These gestures communicate value and affection, keeping hearts tender and connected. Proverbs 16:24 reminds us, "Gracious words are a honeycomb, sweet to the soul and healing to the bones." Proactive love is a daily choice that builds a reservoir of intimacy, making the marriage resistant to silent drift.

Key Principle

Early intervention is not dramatic—it is deliberate.

By noticing subtle signs and responding with prayer, spiritual alignment, and proactive love, couples can reverse drift before it hardens into disconnection.

Prophetic Insight

God often speaks through the quiet signals of drift—moments of disconnection, emotional coldness, or repeated misunderstandings. These subtle whispers are not signs of abandonment but invitations to correction.

When couples respond proactively, they demonstrate obedience and humility, creating fertile ground for divine intervention.

Jesus warned in Matthew 19:8 that hardness of heart is the root of broken covenant. Yet when couples choose to recognise early drift and take deliberate, faith-filled steps, they protect their marriage from both heart hardening and spiritual attack. Obedience in small things—daily prayer, intentional communication, acts of love—becomes the seedbed for restoration and blessing.

Key Principle: Early drift is reversible. Recognising it and responding with humility, prayer, and intentional love transforms the marriage into a testimony of God's grace and covenant strength.

Reflection Exercises

Identify subtle signs of drift in your marriage. Are there moments of emotional withdrawal, coldness, or frequent misunderstandings? Write them down honestly.

Scripture Anchor: "Catch the foxes for us, the little foxes that spoil the vineyards." (Song of Solomon 2:15)

List two practical steps to reconnect emotionally and spiritually. Examples might include daily affirmations, shared meals, or praying together before bed.

Scripture Anchor: "Encourage one another and build each other up." (1 Thessalonians 5:11)

Commit to a 10-minute daily conversation with your spouse focused on heart alignment. Use this time to share feelings, dreams, and reflections without distraction.

Scripture Anchor: "Let every person be quick to hear, slow to speak, slow to anger." (James 1:19)

Pray together, asking God to reveal hidden pride, offense, or neglect in your hearts. Invite the Holy Spirit to soften areas of hardness and restore tenderness.

Scripture Anchor: "Search me, O God, and know my heart; test me and know my anxious thoughts." (Psalm 139:23)

Prayer

Lord, reveal any early signs of drift in my marriage. Teach me to recognise subtle emotional, spiritual, or relational distance and respond with love, humility, and intentional action. Restore connection, unity, and intimacy before hearts harden. Amen.

Declaration

Our hearts remain soft, tender, and aligned with God. We notice drift early and respond with love, prayer, and action. Our marriage is protected, restored, and united in covenantal grace.

CHAPTER 8

Healing Emotional Wounds Before They Harden

"He heals the broken hearted and binds up their wounds."
— Psalm 147:3

Every marriage experiences challenges—disappointments, misunderstandings, or hurts. These wounds, if unaddressed, gradually hardens the heart, producing bitterness, withdrawal, and relational distance. Jesus' words in Matthew 19:8 remind us that hardness of heart is the root problem behind marital breakdown.

Healing emotional wounds is therefore a spiritual, relational, and practical imperative. When couples address pain early, forgiveness flows, intimacy is restored, and marriages are fortified against future drift or division.

A Story of Emotional Healing

Esther and Daniel entered marriage with love and hope, but over the course of ten years, unresolved offenses quietly accumulated. Daniel often forgot important dates—birthdays, anniversaries, or moments that mattered deeply to Esther. Each forgotten occasion left her feeling unvalued and unseen. In response, Esther began to criticise and withdraw affection, believing that her disappointment would speak louder than her words.

Neither of them realised that every unresolved issue was building an invisible wall between them. What began as small cracks in communication grew into barriers of distance, resentment, and silence. Their marriage was functional, but the joy and intimacy that once defined it had faded.

One day, a mentor spoke a simple but profound truth: "Your marriage will only heal when you heal your hearts." That reminder became a turning point. Esther and Daniel chose to begin intentional acts of healing. They practiced forgiveness, releasing past offenses instead of rehearsing them. They opened dialogue, speaking honestly about hurts and hopes. They embraced emotional honesty, allowing vulnerability to replace defensiveness. And they prayed together, inviting God to soften their hearts and restore unity.

Slowly, the walls began to crumble. Affection returned in small gestures—a touch, a smile, a word of encouragement. Laughter reemerged, filling their home with warmth. Spiritual unity was renewed as they aligned their hearts with God's covenant design. What once seemed irreparable became a testimony of grace: healing their hearts healed their marriage.

Understanding Emotional Wounds

Emotional wounds in marriage are not always visible, but they cut deeply into the heart and soul. They often arise from neglect, offense, or unmet expectations, leaving scars that shape how spouses interact with one another. Left unaddressed, these wounds manifest in destructive patterns:

1. Resentment – Past offenses are carried into present interactions, colouring every word and action. "Love keeps no record of wrongs." (1 Corinthians 13:5)
2. Defensiveness – Instead of responding with love, spouses react to perceived attacks, building walls instead of bridges.
3. Withdrawal – Intimacy and communication are avoided as self-protection, creating emotional distance.

4. Bitterness – Anger and hurt begin to shape thoughts, words, and actions, poisoning the atmosphere of the home.

   "See to it that no root of bitterness springs up and causes trouble." (Hebrews 12:15)

5. Distrust – Confidence in a spouse's love or intentions erodes, leaving suspicion and insecurity in its place.

Spiritual Perspective

From a spiritual standpoint, unhealed emotional wounds are more than relational struggles—they are open doors for attack. The enemy exploits bitterness, unforgiveness, and pride to deepen division, harden hearts, and accelerate relational drift. What begins as a small offense can become a foothold for spiritual oppression if left unresolved.

Yet God offers healing. Through forgiveness, humility, and prayer, couples can close these doors and invite His Spirit to restore tenderness and unity. As Psalm 147:3 declares, "He heals the broken-hearted and binds up their wounds." Emotional healing is not only possible—it is promised when couples surrender their pain to Him.

The Path to Healing

Healing in marriage is not accidental—it requires intention, humility, and divine guidance. When couples choose to walk this path together, they invite God to restore what has been broken and renew covenant love.

Steps Toward Healing and Restoration

Healing begins with honesty. Couples must acknowledge the wounds of the past, identifying hurts and admitting them openly without minimising or hiding them.

Rather than assigning blame, the focus should be on how experiences made each person feel.

This shift from accusation to vulnerability opens the door to deeper understanding. As the psalmist prayed, "Search me, O God, and know my heart; test me and know my anxious thoughts" (Psalm 139:23).

The next step is to forgive deeply. Offenses must be released to God and to one another, choosing freedom over bitterness. Forgiveness does not excuse wrongdoing, but it liberates the heart from captivity and allows healing to begin. Scripture reminds us, "Bear with each other and forgive one another… Forgive as the Lord forgave you" (Colossians 3:13).

Transparent communication is essential. Couples should speak openly about how offenses have affected them, using "I feel" statements rather than accusations. Listening with patience—without interruption, judgment, or defensiveness—creates space for true healing, as James exhorts: "Let every person be quick to hear, slow to speak, slow to anger" (James 1:19).

Trust and intimacy are restored through consistency. Honesty, reliability, and accountability in daily actions rebuild confidence, while emotional closeness grows through shared experiences such as meals, laughter, prayer, and intentional affection. Ecclesiastes reminds us of the strength found in unity: "Two are better than one… If either of them falls down, one can help the other up" (Ecclesiastes 4:9–10).

Finally, couples must invite God's healing. Prayer, both individually and together, asking the Lord to restore hearts and renew unity. Declaring scripture affirmations over the marriage—such as "By His stripes, our hearts are healed" (Isaiah 53:5)—anchors the process in God's covenantal design. Healing is not only emotional but deeply spiritual, rooted in His plan for marriage.

Key Principle

Healing is a journey of humility and faith. When couples acknowledge wounds, forgive deeply, communicate transparently, restore trust, and invite God's healing, they dismantle walls of division and rebuild a marriage anchored in grace and covenant love.

Illustrations of Healing

The Marriage Repaired

Naomi and Peter carried unspoken grievances for years, each silently nursing hurts that built invisible walls between them. When they finally set aside time to confess, forgive, and pray, something shifted. Within weeks, emotional barriers softened, laughter returned to their home, and intimacy was renewed. Their story shows that confession and forgiveness are powerful tools for dismantling walls of resentment.

Healing Through Prayer and Devotion

Lydia and Samuel found themselves caught in recurring cycles of conflict. Instead of allowing frustration to define their marriage, they committed to praying together daily for three consecutive weeks, asking God to heal hidden pain. As they sought Him, emotional barriers broke, and their connection deepened. Their testimony reflects the truth of Matthew 18:20: "For where two or three are gathered in my name, there am I among them."

Restoration Through Acts of Love

Maria and Daniel discovered that healing doesn't always require grand gestures—it often comes through small, intentional acts. Words of affirmation, gentle touch, and serving one another in daily life accelerated their healing process.

These simple acts reinforced trust and created emotional safety, reminding them that love expressed consistently is a powerful antidote to drift.

Prophetic Insight

God is the ultimate healer of hearts. His grace reaches into places of brokenness that human effort alone cannot mend. When couples choose to acknowledge wounds rather than hide them, they bring hidden pain into the light where healing can begin. When they forgive proactively instead of rehearsing offenses, they release bitterness and open the door for reconciliation.

And when they invite His presence into the healing process through prayer and devotion, they allow the Spirit of God to restore unity and renew covenant love.

In this way, trust and intimacy are not rebuilt by technique alone but by surrendering to the One who makes all things new. What was fractured becomes whole, and what appeared to be beyond repair becomes a testimony of divine restoration.

Healing is not merely emotional—it is spiritual. When couples surrender their pain to God, He softens hardened hearts, restores intimacy, and renews covenant love.

Key Principle

Unhealed wounds harden hearts, creating fertile ground for divorce or prolonged conflict. Healing before hardening preserves intimacy, restores trust, and aligns the marriage with God's original design.

Couples who respond early with humility, forgiveness, and prayer discover that God's grace is more than enough to rebuild what seemed broken beyond repair.

Practical Exercises for Couples

Identify One Unresolved Emotional Wound

- Take time to reflect on past hurts that may still linger.
- Pray honestly, confessing the wound to God, and then share it vulnerably with your spouse.
- Scripture Anchor: "He heals the broken-hearted and binds up their wounds." (Psalm 147:3)

Commit to Forgive Daily

- Choose forgiveness even for small offenses, refusing to let bitterness take root.
- Remember that forgiveness is not about excusing behaviour—it's about freeing your heart from captivity.
- Scripture Anchor: "Forgive as the Lord forgave you." (Colossians 3:13)

Engage in One Act of Intentional Love Per Day

- Show love through simple, consistent actions: a kind word, a gentle touch, a thoughtful gesture.
- These daily acts rebuild emotional closeness and remind your spouse of their value.
- Scripture Anchor: "Let us not love with words or speech but with actions and in truth." (1 John 3:18)

Share Positive Affirmations and Gratitude Weekly

- Set aside time each week to affirm your spouse's strengths and express gratitude for their presence in your life.
- Gratitude shifts focus from flaws to blessings, strengthening trust and intimacy.

- Scripture Anchor: "Encourage one another and build each other up." (1 Thessalonians 5:11)

Key Principle

Healing and restoration in marriage are cultivated through small, consistent acts of love, forgiveness, and gratitude. When couples practice these exercises faithfully, they invite God's presence into their relationship and strengthen the covenant bond that holds them together.

Prayer

Lord, heal the emotional wounds in my marriage. Remove every trace of bitterness, resentment, and offense. Restore trust, intimacy, and love between me and my spouse.
May our hearts remain tender and aligned with Your covenant plan. Amen.

Declaration

"Our hearts are healed by God's grace. Emotional wounds are restored, intimacy is renewed, and love flows freely. Hardness has no place in our marriage. We walk in unity, forgiveness, and covenantal joy."

CHAPTER 9

Restoring Communication: Words That Heal, Not Harm

"Death and life are in the power of the tongue, and those who love it will eat its fruits."
— Proverbs 18:21

The Power of Communication in Marriage

Communication is the lifeblood of marriage. Words carry the power to either nurture intimacy, trust, and unity—or to erect walls, deepen resentment, and harden hearts. Many marriages do not collapse because love has disappeared, but because communication has become destructive. Silence, criticism, or harsh words slowly erode the foundation of covenant love.

Jesus' words in Matthew 19:8 reminds us that hardness of heart undermines marriage at its root. That hardness often grows from words left unspoken—needs ignored, feelings suppressed—or words spoken in anger that wound rather than heal. Over time, these patterns create distance that love alone cannot bridge.

Restoring healthy communication is therefore essential for both emotional and spiritual restoration. When couples choose to speak with honesty, humility, and gentleness, they invite healing into their relationship. Words of affirmation rebuild trust. Transparent dialogue dismantles walls. Prayerful conversation re-centre the marriage in God's presence.

Healthy communication is not simply about talking—it is about listening, understanding, and responding with love.

As Proverbs 18:21 declares, "The tongue has the power of life and death." Couples who use their words to speak life discover that communication becomes not a weapon of division, but a channel of grace and unity.

What Silent Treatment Really Means

The silent treatment is not simply "taking space." It is often a form of passive-aggressive behaviour where one partner withdraws communication to punish or manipulate. While silence can sometimes be healthy when used for cooling down or reflection, the silent treatment differs because it intentionally creates distance and tension. Over time, this pattern breeds confusion, isolation, and despair in the recipient, who feels unheard, dismissed, and devalued. It communicates a powerful negative message: "You don't matter to me." Such rejection hardens hearts, erodes trust, and undermines the covenant of marriage, which is built on openness, love, and mutual respect.

Healthy relationships thrive on honest dialogue, forgiveness, and reconciliation. When communication is withheld as a weapon, it damages intimacy and prevents healing. Instead of silence, couples are called to speak truth in love, even when it is difficult, so that unity can be restored.

Scripture Anchor: "Do not let the sun go down while you are still angry, and do not give the devil a foothold." (Ephesians 4:26–27)

What Communication Breakdown Really Means in Marriage

In a marriage, communication is more than talking—it's about connection, trust, and emotional safety. A breakdown occurs when dialogue shifts from openness to defensiveness, silence, or misunderstanding. This doesn't mean couples stop speaking altogether; rather, the quality of communication erodes.

Partners may talk about logistics—bills, schedules, chores—but avoid deeper conversations about feelings, needs, or dreams. Over time, this creates distance and resentment.

Research shows that poor communication is one of the most common sources of marital conflict, often leading to frustration, emotional withdrawal, and even divorce if left unaddressed. Common causes include stress, assumptions, defensiveness, or the belief that a spouse should "just know" what the other feels. These patterns quietly poison intimacy and trust.

Is Breakdown a Myth?

Some argue that communication never truly "breaks down" because couples are always sending messages—through silence, tone, or body language. In this sense, communication continues, but it becomes distorted or destructive. The myth lies in thinking that breakdown means no communication at all. In reality, what breaks down is healthy, constructive communication.

Why It Matters

- Emotional impact: One partner feels ignored or misunderstood, while the other may feel overwhelmed or unheard.
- Spiritual impact: Silence or harsh words undermine unity and covenant.
- Practical impact: Misunderstandings about finances, parenting, or priorities grow into conflict.

Healthy marriages require intentional listening, empathy, and vulnerability. When couples recognise the signs of breakdown—withdrawal, constant arguments, or silence—they can rebuild by practicing patience, asking clarifying questions, and committing to daily heart-to-heart conversations.

Scripture Anchor

"Let your conversation be always full of grace, seasoned with salt, so that you may know how to answer everyone." (Colossians 4:6)

This verse reminds couples that communication should be gracious, thoughtful, and intentional, fostering understanding rather than division.

Emotional and Relational Effects of Silence in Marriage

Silence in marriage does more than pause conversation—it damages intimacy by blocking emotional connection and making spouses feel like strangers. When communication is withheld, trust begins to erode, weakening the foundation of confidence in the relationship. Hurt that is left unspoken often grows into resentment, which hardens the heart and creates bitterness. Instead of resolving issues, the silent treatment escalates tension and prolongs conflict, trapping both partners in a cycle of misunderstanding.

In its most harmful form, prolonged silence can even become a form of emotional abuse when used to control or punish, leaving deep wounds that are difficult to heal. Marriage is designed to thrive on openness, forgiveness, and mutual encouragement. Silence, when used as a weapon, undermines the covenant and prevents reconciliation.

Scripture reminds us of the power of words to heal and restore: "Gracious words are a honeycomb, sweet to the soul and healing to the bones." (Proverbs 16:24). Choosing to speak with love, even in moments of hurt, opens the door for healing and strengthens the bond of unity.

Path Toward Healing

Healing in marriage begins with breaking the cycle of silence and choosing instead to engage in gentle, honest communication. When words are spoken in humility and kindness, they open the door for reconciliation and restore emotional connection. Seeking understanding is equally vital; rather than casting blame or accusations, couples can use "I feel" statements to express their hearts in ways that invite empathy and compassion.

Forgiveness must also be practiced daily. Releasing offenses quickly prevents bitterness from taking root and allows love to flourish even in moments of weakness. True healing is not found in human effort alone but in God's presence. When couples pray together, they invite the Holy Spirit to soften hardened hearts, restore tenderness, and renew unity. In this sacred space, wounds can be mended, trust rebuilt, and intimacy restored.

Scripture reminds us of this divine partnership: "Be kind and compassionate to one another, forgiving each other, just as in Christ God forgave you." (Ephesians 4:32).

Key Principle

Silent treatment is not harmless—it is destructive. Healing requires humility, intentional communication, and spiritual alignment to restore intimacy and protect the marriage covenant.

Silent Treatment vs. Healthy Silence

Silent treatment itself is generally harmful, but short, intentional silence—when used wisely—can have limited positives. The key difference lies in whether silence is used as punishment, which is destructive, or as space for reflection, which can be constructive.

While the silent treatment as emotional withdrawal damages intimacy and trust, healthy silence can serve a meaningful purpose. Taking a pause before conflict escalates can prevent hurtful words spoken in anger.

Creating space for reflection allows both partners to process emotions and think clearly before responding. A short period of quiet can also help avoid reactive communication, enabling couples to respond with care and empathy rather than frustration.

Silence, when shared intentionally, can even deepen emotional closeness. Sitting together peacefully without words can foster non-verbal connection, while attentive listening during moments of quiet allows one partner to speak fully and the other to truly understand.

The critical distinction is clear. Silent treatment is negative—it is withdrawal used as punishment, manipulation, or control, leading to confusion, isolation, resentment, and even emotional abuse. Healthy silence, on the other hand, is positive—it is a deliberate pause to reflect, pray, or calm emotions before re-engaging in constructive dialogue.

When followed by open communication, this kind of silence strengthens trust, nurtures intimacy, and restores unity.

Scripture reminds us of the wisdom in measured words and thoughtful pauses: "A gentle answer turns away wrath, but a harsh word stirs up anger." (Proverbs 15:1).

Key Principle

Silence can be healing when it is brief, intentional, and followed by honest communication. Used wisely, it allows space for reflection and calm. But when silence is used to punish or manipulate, it becomes destructive, eroding trust and intimacy. Couples must learn to distinguish between healthy pauses that lead back to connection and harmful withdrawal that creates division.

"A time to keep silence, and a time to speak." (Ecclesiastes 3:7)

A Story of Words That Wounded

Esther and Peter's marriage began with love and promise, but over time small disagreements grew into patterns of poor communication. When Esther shared her concerns, Peter often responded with sarcasm or dismissal, leaving her feeling minimised and unseen. In turn, Esther began to withdraw emotionally, retreating into silence that created even greater distance between them.

Arguments rarely ended in resolution. Instead, they dissolved into cold silence, deepening the emotional walls that separated them. What had started as a covenant of intimacy was slowly being reshaped into a cycle of resentment and disconnection, driven not by dramatic betrayals but by the steady erosion of trust through words and silence.

The Turning Point of Restoration

As the silence between them grew heavier, Esther and Peter reached a sobering realisation: their marriage could not survive without change.

They began to see that communication was not neutral—it was shaping the very atmosphere of their relationship. Sarcasm had hardened their hearts, and silence had built emotional walls.

Determined to break the cycle, they chose to relearn how to speak to one another. Peter began pausing before responding, replacing sarcasm with gentleness. Esther found courage to express her feelings openly rather than retreating into silence. Together, they committed to listening with patience, speaking with clarity, and anchoring their words in love.

Slowly, the atmosphere shifted. Grace softened their tone. Clarity opened understanding. Love rebuilt trust. What once felt like a covenant unravelling was restored into a bond of tenderness and intimacy. Their journey proved the truth of Proverbs 18:21: "The tongue has the power of life and death, and those who love it will eat its fruit."

Neither of them realised at first that their words—or lack of them—were shaping the reality of their marriage. Sarcasm hardened hearts. Silence created emotional walls. What was meant to be a covenant of intimacy was slowly becoming a cycle of resentment and disconnection.

Eventually, they came to a sobering realisation: communication was not neutral. Words had the power to either destroy or restore. They chose to relearn how to speak—with grace instead of sarcasm, with clarity instead of dismissal, and with love instead of silence.

As they practiced new patterns of communication, connection began to return. Grace softened their tone. Clarity opened understanding. Love rebuilt trust. Slowly, the atmosphere of their marriage shifted from tension to tenderness, proving the truth of Proverbs 18:21: "The tongue has the power of life and death, and those who love it will eat its fruit."

Reflection

This story illustrates that communication is not just about exchanging words—it is about shaping the spiritual and emotional climate of a marriage. Every word spoken carry weight, either building intimacy or eroding trust.

Couples who choose grace-filled communication invite God's presence into their relationship, transforming conflict into connection and resentment into restoration.

The Impact of Words in Marriage

Words carry extraordinary power in shaping the atmosphere of a marriage. They can heal or they can wound. When spoken with love, encouragement restores confidence and emotional safety, apologies and affirmations foster reconciliation, and scripture and prayer reinforce both love and spiritual alignment. These life-giving words nurture intimacy and strengthen the covenant bond.

On the other hand, words can also wound deeply. Criticism, sarcasm, and blame build resentment, while repeated negative statements reinforce emotional walls. Silence or avoidance communicates rejection and disengagement, leaving one partner feeling unseen and unloved. Over time, these destructive patterns harden hearts and erode trust.

The truth is simple yet profound: hard hearts often begin with unhealed wounds expressed through harmful words. Changing the way couples communicate—choosing grace over sarcasm, affirmation over criticism, and openness over silence—can soften hearts and prevent marital drift, restoring unity and intimacy in the relationship.

Practical Steps to Restoring Healthy Communication

Healthy communication in marriage requires intentionality, humility, and a commitment to love. One of the most powerful practices is speaking with intentional love—pausing before responding, especially in moments of conflict, and asking yourself whether your words will build your spouse up or tear them down. This simple discipline transforms conversations from reactive to restorative.

Listening actively is equally vital. Giving full attention when your spouse speaks, reflecting back what you've heard, and resisting the urge to interrupt or prepare a rebuttal communicates respect and understanding. It assures your spouse that their voice matters and their feelings are valued.

Couples must also learn to avoid accusatory language. Replacing phrases like "You always…" with "I feel…" shifts the focus from blame to vulnerability. Expressing emotions rather than accusations opens the door to empathy and connection.

Daily affirmations strengthen the bond further. Words of appreciation, gratitude, and encouragement highlight your spouse's efforts, qualities, and contributions, reinforcing emotional safety and trust.

Conflict, when left unresolved, festers into bitterness. Addressing misunderstandings quickly, forgiving readily, and seeking mutual understanding rather than victory ensures that disagreements become opportunities for growth rather than division.

Finally, scripture and prayer should be woven into dialogue. God's Word provides encouragement and guidance, while praying together invites His presence into the conversation. Prayer softens hearts, cultivates humility, and restores clarity, ensuring that communication remains anchored in covenant love.

Illustrations of Restored Communication

Rachel and David had been silent for weeks after a painful disagreement. Recognising the distance between them, they scheduled time to pray together and then speak honestly about their feelings. By listening without judgment, forgiveness began to flow, and their connection deepened. What once felt like a wall of silence became a doorway to renewed intimacy.

Mark and Lydia discovered the healing power of daily affirmation. They committed to speaking three affirming words to each other every day. Over the course of months, this simple habit softened their hearts, prevented emotional drift, and strengthened their intimacy.

Their marriage was transformed not by grand gestures, but by consistent words of encouragement that acted like daily medicine for the soul.

Samuel and Hannah faced recurring arguments about chores, but instead of continuing the cycle of blame, they chose a new approach. They began expressing their feelings and needs respectfully, focusing on understanding rather than winning. This shift turned conflict into opportunities for connection, allowing them to grow closer even in the midst of disagreements.

These stories highlight that communication, when guided by grace, prayer, and intentional love, has the power to restore intimacy and transform conflict into closeness.

Prophetic Insight

God created words as instruments of life. They were never meant to be casual or careless, but carriers of His Spirit and His truth. When spoken with love, patience, and humility, words have the power to soften hardened hearts, repair emotional wounds, and restore spiritual unity within marriage. They become seeds of healing, planting grace and reconciliation where division once grew.

Yet words left unhealed—those spoken in anger, sarcasm, or silence—do not simply fade away. They linger, strengthening bitterness, pride, and hardness of heart. The enemy exploits these unhealed words to sow discord, creating distance where God intended intimacy.

Key Principle:

Restoring communication is not just technique—it is a spiritual act. Words spoken with grace align hearts with God's covenant, creating space for love, forgiveness, and intimacy. When couples invite the Holy Spirit into their conversations, dialogue becomes healing, worship, and a testimony of grace.

Reflection Exercises

Restoring communication begins with intentional reflection. Start by identifying the words or phrases you often use that may wound your spouse.

Once recognised, commit to replacing them with affirming language that builds rather than tears down. This shift in speech transforms the atmosphere of your marriage from criticism to encouragement.

Set aside a daily 15-minute conversation devoted not to tasks or logistics, but to sharing feelings, expressing gratitude, or praying together. These moments of intentional connection nurture emotional intimacy and remind both spouses that their relationship is rooted in covenant love.

Take time to reflect on past conflicts and consider how words could have healed rather than hurt.

Writing these insights down helps you recognise patterns and equips you to respond differently in the future, turning potential arguments into opportunities for understanding.

Finally, pray together, asking God to guide your tongue and soften your hearts. Prayer sanctifies communication, ensuring that words are not merely exchanged but infused with grace, humility, and love.

Prayer

Lord, teach us to communicate with love, grace, and wisdom. Remove every word that wound, and let every word build, heal, and restore. Guide our conversations, soften our hearts, and strengthen our marriage covenant. Amen.

Declaration

"Our words heal, our hearts are tender, and our marriage thrives in love, grace, and unity. Communication flows with understanding, patience, and encouragement. Hardness has no place in our home."

CHAPTER 10

Restoring Trust: The Cornerstone of Lasting Marriages

"It always protects, always trusts, always hopes, always perseveres."
– 1 Corinthians 13:7

Trust: The Foundation of Marriage

Trust is the bedrock of any lasting marriage. Without it, love becomes fragile, communication falters, and emotional walls begin to rise. Even a single act of betrayal, a repeated offense, or a broken promise can chip away at trust, leaving cracks that harden the heart and weaken the covenant bond.

Yet trust, though delicate, is not beyond repair. Restoring it is not easy—but it is possible. Like rebuilding a wall brick by brick, it requires humility to admit wrongs, transparency to live openly, forgiveness to release offenses, and spiritual guidance to anchor the process in God's grace.

When couples commit to this journey, trust can be rebuilt stronger than before. Each act of honesty becomes a brick. Each moment of forgiveness becomes mortar. Each prayer for healing becomes a safeguard against future fractures. Over time, the wall of trust rises again, not as a fragile structure, but as a fortified foundation for love, intimacy, and unity.

Key Principle:

Trust is not restored by words alone but by consistent actions, humility, and reliance on God's Spirit.

As Proverbs 3:5–6 reminds us, "Trust in the Lord with all your heart and lean not on your own understanding; in all your ways submit to Him, and He will make your paths straight." When couples place their trust in God first, He empowers them to rebuild trust with one another.

A Story of Broken and Restored Trust

James and Naomi had built their marriage on love and shared dreams, but years into their journey Naomi discovered that James had withheld a significant truth about their finances. The revelation struck her deeply. Feeling betrayed, her heart hardened, and emotional distance began to grow. Affection faded, suspicion coloured every word James spoke, and arguments escalated until the atmosphere of their home was tense and heavy.

Instead of giving up, James chose a different path. He acknowledged his wrongdoing without excuses, humbly admitting the pain his actions had caused. He opened every financial detail to Naomi, choosing transparency over secrecy. He committed himself to daily accountability and open communication, proving through consistent actions that he was determined to rebuild what had been broken.

Over time, Naomi's heart began to soften. The walls of suspicion gave way to renewed trust, and emotional intimacy returned. Their marriage, once fractured, became stronger than before—rebuilt on honesty, forgiveness, and divine guidance. What had threatened to destroy them became the very thing God used to deepen their covenant bond.

This story beautifully illustrates that trust can be broken in a moment but restored through humility, transparency, and consistency.

Understanding Trust in Marriage

Trust in marriage is both relational and spiritual, forming the foundation upon which love and intimacy are built. At its core, trust begins with faith in your spouse's integrity—believing that their words and actions align with the promises they have made. This confidence allows couples to rest in the assurance that honesty and commitment guide their relationship.

Trust also grows through reliance on consistent character. When actions consistently match words over time, reliability becomes a safeguard against doubt. Each act of faithfulness, no matter how small, strengthens the bond and reinforces the stability of the marriage.

Equally important is openness and vulnerability. True trust creates a safe space where couples can share fears, dreams, and weaknesses without fear of judgment. Vulnerability invites intimacy, reminding each spouse that they are fully seen and yet fully loved.

Finally, trust in marriage is deeply spiritual. Beyond human effort, it requires dependence on God to guide and protect the covenant, even when mistakes occur. Trusting Him ensures that the marriage is anchored not only in human promises but in divine faithfulness, which never fails.

The Consequences of Broken Trust

When trust is broken in marriage, the effects ripple through every part of the relationship. Emotional withdrawal often occurs, leaving one or both spouses feeling distant and disconnected. Communication becomes defensive or guarded, as words are filtered through suspicion rather than openness. Resentment and bitterness begin to grow, slowly eroding affection and goodwill.

Over time, hearts harden, increasing vulnerability to conflict and creating the conditions for marital drift.

Jesus' warning about hardened hearts in Matthew 19:8 reminds us that breaches of trust, if left unaddressed, can ultimately threaten the covenant itself. Trust is not simply a relational bond—it is a spiritual safeguard. When it is broken, couples must act quickly and humbly to repair it, lest the enemy use that fracture to sow division.

Pathway to Healing Broken Trust

Acknowledge the Breach

Healing begins with honesty. The offending spouse must admit the wrongdoing without excuses or minimising truth. Naming the hurt validates the pain and opens the door to reconciliation.

Practice Transparency

Trust cannot be rebuilt in secrecy. Share details openly—whether about finances, communication, or daily habits. Transparency demonstrates a willingness to live in the light and removes suspicion.

Commit to Consistency

Words alone are not enough; actions must align with promises. Consistent behaviour over time rebuilds reliability. Each act of integrity becomes a brick in the wall of restored trust.

Extend Forgiveness

The wounded spouse must choose forgiveness, even if emotions take time to catch up. Forgiveness does not erase the offense but releases bitterness, allowing healing to begin.

Invite Accountability

Healthy trust often requires outside support. This may include mentors, counsellors, or trusted friends who help ensure commitments are kept. Accountability strengthens the process and prevents relapse.

Rebuild Emotional Intimacy

As trust grows, couples should intentionally nurture closeness—through affection, affirmation, and shared experiences. Emotional intimacy restores the warmth that betrayal once stole.

Anchor in Spiritual Guidance

Ultimately, trust is sustained by God's grace. Couples must pray together, seek His wisdom, and rely on His Spirit to soften hearts. Scripture reminds us that "Love always protects, always trusts, always hopes, always perseveres" (1 Corinthians 13:7).

Key Principle:

Restoring trust is not a quick fix but a journey. With humility, transparency, forgiveness, and God's guidance, broken trust can be rebuilt stronger than before, transforming wounds into testimonies of grace.

Illustrations of Trust Restoration

Peter and Hannah faced the pain of emotional betrayal, and for a time their marriage appeared fragile. Yet through months of consistent honesty, accountability, and prayer, trust was slowly rebuilt. What began as brokenness became a testimony of resilience, and their marriage emerged stronger than before, fortified by grace and perseverance.

Lydia and Samuel struggled with secrecy and suspicion that threatened to erode their bond. Choosing a new path, they began praying together daily, sharing vulnerabilities openly, and practicing transparency in all matters. As they invited God into their partnership, trust and intimacy returned, transforming their relationship into a spiritual union marked by openness and faith.

Rachel carried hesitation in her heart after Daniel's repeated offenses, unsure if trust could ever be restored. But by practicing forgiveness daily and focusing on God's faithfulness rather than her pain, she released resentment. In doing so, she opened the door for trust and love to flourish anew, proving that forgiveness can be the catalyst for restoration.

These stories highlight three key pathways to rebuilding trust: consistent honesty, spiritual partnership, and daily forgiveness.

Each demonstrates that while trust may be fragile, it can be restored through intentional choices and reliance on God's guidance.

Prophetic Insight

God is the ultimate restorer of trust. Though human hearts falter, His grace softens even the hardest places, bringing healing where betrayal has wounded and renewing unity where covenant has been fractured. Trust is not rebuilt overnight; it requires honesty, humility, and spiritual alignment. Yet under God's guidance, what was once fragile becomes resilient—fortified by grace and sustained by His faithfulness.

Key Principle:

Trust restored through God's Spirit is not merely repaired—it is transformed.

It becomes a testimony of His power to redeem brokenness and to turn weakness into strength, ensuring that covenant love endures.

Reflection Exercises

Begin by prayerfully identifying one area where trust has been weakened in your marriage. Naming the wound is the first step toward healing, as it brings hidden pains into the light.

Next, consider three daily actions you can take to restore transparency and reliability. These may include sharing details openly, following through on promises, or practicing accountability in small matters. Consistency in these actions will slowly rebuild confidence.

Commit together to daily prayers of forgiveness and spiritual alignment. As you invite God into your communication, His Spirit softens hearts, releases bitterness, and strengthens covenant love.

Finally, speak affirmations over your marriage. Declare unity, love, and covenantal trust aloud, reminding one another that your bond is not defined by past failures but by God's faithfulness and your shared commitment to restoration.

Prayer

Lord, restore trust in my marriage. Heal wounds of betrayal, strengthen our hearts, and guide us in transparency, honesty, and accountability. May our covenant remain unbroken, and our hearts fully aligned in love and unity. Amen.

Declaration

"Our marriage is built on trust, transparency, and covenantal love. Betrayal, doubt, and offense have no place in our home. Our hearts are aligned, our spirits united, and our love restored through God's grace."

CHAPTER 11

Guarding the Heart Against Future Drift

"Above all else, guard your heart, for everything you do flows from it."
— Proverbs 4:23

Marriage thrives when hearts remain soft, tender, and aligned with God. But even after healing and restoration, the danger of drift remains. Life pressures, spiritual attacks, and human tendencies toward pride or neglect can slowly harden hearts again if couples are not vigilant.

Guarding the heart is not optional—it is a spiritual, relational, and practical discipline that safeguards love, trust, and intimacy.

A Story of Vigilance

Consider the marriage of Ruth and Elijah. After facing years of conflict and near separation, they made a deliberate commitment to heart-level restoration. They began praying together regularly, sharing their feelings openly, and celebrating even the smallest victories in communication and emotional connection. Whenever challenges arose, they sought spiritual counsel, refusing to let difficulties linger unaddressed.

Because they actively guarded their hearts, Ruth and Elijah avoided relapse into bitterness, resentment, and emotional withdrawal. Their marriage became a living testimony of proactive vigilance and covenantal alignment, showing that restoration is not a one-time event but a daily choice to protect love and nurture unity.

Understanding Heart Guarding

Guarding the heart is about protecting your emotions, thoughts, and spirit from influences that can cause drift or hardening. It is both a spiritual and relational discipline, requiring intentional awareness and daily practice.

At its core, heart guarding begins with spiritual awareness. The heart is a battlefield, and pride, unforgiveness, and negativity can invite spiritual attacks that weaken unity. Recognising this reality helps couples remain vigilant, choosing humility and grace as their defence.

It also requires emotional stewardship. This means monitoring your thoughts, feelings, and reactions toward your spouse, and addressing emotional hurt before it escalates into hardness. By tending to emotions early, couples prevent small wounds from becoming deep fractures.

Finally, heart guarding involves relational discipline. Open communication, consistent affection, and mutual respect create a safe environment where love can thrive. Boundaries must also be set against habits or situations that undermine unity, ensuring that the marriage remains protected and aligned with God's covenantal design.

Practical Steps to Guard the Heart

Guarding the heart begins with daily self-reflection. Each morning is an opportunity to examine whether pride, offense, or resentment have taken root. By bringing these attitudes before God in prayer, couples can ask for hearts that are soft, tender, and obedient to His will.

Spiritual connection must also be prioritised. Couples who pray and worship together consistently invite God's presence into their relationship. Studying scripture as a couple and meditating on His covenant for marriage strengthens the spiritual foundation that sustains unity.

Emotional transparency is equally vital. Sharing feelings, concerns, and joys regularly ensures that communication remains open and honest.

Addressing small misunderstandings immediately prevents them from escalating into larger conflicts, keeping hearts free from unnecessary hardness.

Love and unity are celebrated through daily affirmations and intentional joy. Acknowledging and appreciating each other's contributions nurtures gratitude, while creating moments of laughter, shared experiences, and affection strengthens the bond of intimacy.

Finally, couples must guard against external threats. Protecting the marriage from gossip, temptations, or unsupportive relationships preserves its integrity. Seeking counsel and accountability when challenges arise provides wisdom and reinforcement, ensuring that the marriage remains aligned with God's design.

Illustrations of Heart Guarding

Sarah and Michael chose to practice proactive communication by implementing weekly "heart check-ins." These intentional conversations allowed them to consistently share their feelings and catch subtle emotional drift early, preventing relational gaps from forming.

Naomi and Daniel recognised that external pressures were beginning to affect their marriage. In response, they turned to spiritual defence, committing themselves to daily prayer, fasting, and scripture meditation. By doing so, they fortified their hearts against bitterness and pride, ensuring that their relationship remained anchored in God's strength.

James and Rebecca embraced the discipline of celebrating love. They committed to monthly date nights and spoke daily affirmations over one another. These intentional acts of joy and appreciation reinforced emotional intimacy and kept their hearts tender, preventing hardness from taking root.

Prophetic Insight

God entrusts couples with the sacred duty of guarding their hearts. Restoration is not a single event but an ongoing covenant that requires vigilance and intentionality.

When couples remain watchful, they invite divine protection, build resilience against trials, and preserve love, trust, and unity—allowing their marriage to flourish in strength and tenderness.

Key Principle:

A marriage thrives when couples actively guard their hearts, maintaining obedience to God and covenantal alignment with His design.

Reflection Exercises

Begin by identifying potential sources of heart drift in your marriage. Naming these influences—whether they stem from busyness, unresolved conflict, or external pressures—brings awareness to areas that need protection and care.

Commit to daily spiritual and emotional practices that guard your heart. Prayer, scripture meditation, and intentional acts of kindness create a rhythm that keeps love tender and aligned with God's will.

Establish a weekly routine of intentional connection.

Set aside time for prayer, meaningful communication, and shared activities that nurture intimacy. These practices strengthen unity and remind both spouses of the covenant they share.

Finally, pray together, asking God to continuously soften your hearts and preserve unity. Inviting His presence into your marriage ensures that restoration is not temporary but sustained by divine grace.

Prayer

Lord, help us guard our hearts against hardness, pride, and neglect. Protect our marriage from drift and spiritual attack. Keep our hearts tender, our spirits aligned, and our love strong. Amen.

Declaration

"We guard our hearts daily. Hardness, resentment, and emotional withdrawal have no place in our marriage. Love, unity, and covenantal faithfulness flow continuously in our home."

CHAPTER 12

Cultivating Daily Practices That Keep Hearts Soft

"Create in me a clean heart, O God, and renew a right spirit within me."
— Psalm 51:10

Soft Hearts, Resilient Marriages

Soft hearts are fertile soil where love, intimacy, and unity can flourish. They welcome tenderness, invite connection, and create space for covenantal trust to deepen. Hard hearts, on the other hand, become the breeding ground for bitterness, pride, and marital drift. When left unchecked, they erect walls that isolate spouses and weaken the bond God intended to be unbreakable.

The difference between a soft heart and a hardened one lies in daily choices. Spiritual, emotional, and relational practices are essential to maintain tenderness and prevent hardness from creeping in unnoticed. Prayer, forgiveness, intentional communication, and acts of love are not occasional remedies but consistent disciplines that keep hearts aligned with God's design.

This chapter explores practical, consistent habits couples can adopt to nurture soft hearts and resilient marriages. It is a call to vigilance, reminding us that love is sustained not by chance but by covenantal commitment, daily devotion, and the grace of God working within us.

A Story of Daily Heart Care

Consider the marriage of Lydia and Samuel. After years of conflict and reconciliation, they came to understand that restoration is not a one-time event but a daily process. To nurture their relationship, they began to implement small, intentional practices that shaped the rhythm of their lives together. Each morning, they prayed side by side, setting the tone for their day with God's presence. At midday, whether through a short call or a shared meal, they offered words of affirmation to one another, reminding each other of their love and value.

Once a week, they set aside time for heart-level check-ins, discussing their feelings, challenges, and gratitude with openness and humility. At night, before closing their day, they read scripture together, reinforcing their spiritual alignment and anchoring their marriage in God's covenant.

Over time, these daily practices became their spiritual heartbeat. They kept Lydia and Samuel's hearts soft, tender, and aligned with God's design, transforming their marriage into a living testimony of consistent care and intentional devotion.

Daily Practices to Keep Hearts Soft

Morning devotion and prayer set the tone for the day. By beginning each morning with God, couples invite His presence to guard their hearts, soften their spirits, and align their relationship with His will. These moments of shared devotion become the foundation upon which tenderness and unity are built.

The Long-Term Impact of Daily Practices

Daily habits do more than keep hearts soft in the moment—they shape the culture of the marriage over time. When couples consistently engage in prayer, affirmation, and emotional transparency, their relationship develops resilience against life pressures such as work stress, parenting challenges, or extended family conflict.

They also gain strength to withstand spiritual attacks that target emotional vulnerability, mistrust, or bitterness. Even emotional fatigue, which can otherwise lead to withdrawal or resentment, is overcome through the steady rhythm of intentional practices.

Soft hearts become fertile ground for intimacy—physical, emotional, and spiritual. Couples who maintain these daily disciplines often discover that connection, laughter, and affection are not occasional experiences but the natural rhythm of their married life.

Encouraging Example

Consider Lydia and Samuel once more. Over the years, they committed to simple daily practices: morning prayer, evening reflection, affirmations, and small acts of kindness. Minor disagreements no longer escalated into arguments, emotional walls never had the chance to form, and their hearts remained tender and responsive. Their home became a place of spiritual peace, emotional warmth, and mutual encouragement, reflecting God's covenantal design for marriage.

This illustrates a key truth: soft hearts lead to marriages that are vibrant, protected, and aligned with God's purpose. Soft hearts are not accidental—they are cultivated. Each prayer, each affirmation, and each act of kindness is a brick in the foundation of a marriage designed to withstand adversity.

Couples who prioritise these daily spiritual and emotional practices are not only preventing hardness of heart—they are creating a legacy of love, unity, and covenantal faithfulness.

Reflection Exercise

Choose one practice from today's teaching to implement consistently for the next thirty days. Let this discipline become part of your daily rhythm, shaping the way you connect and care for one another. At the end of each week, take time to reflect together on how this practice is affecting your hearts and interactions. Notice the changes, however small, and celebrate the growth that comes from intentional effort.

As you continue, pray for divine reinforcement. Ask God to make these practices natural, life-giving, and spiritually protective. In doing so, you invite His Spirit to strengthen your marriage, ensuring that tenderness, unity, and covenantal love remain at the centre of your relationship.

Prayer

Lord, help us not only begin our days with You but walk each moment intentionally toward love, tenderness, and unity. Let our hearts remain soft, our words life-giving, and our marriage reflect Your covenantal glory. Protect us from hardness of heart, pride, and drift, and keep our union vibrant and strong for all seasons. Amen.

Declaration

"We cultivate soft hearts through daily devotion, affirmation, and love. Our marriage thrives in grace, peace, and unity. Hardness, bitterness, and division have no place in our home. We walk together in covenantal love and spiritual alignment."

CHAPTER 13

Maintaining Intimacy and Emotional Connection Through Life's Seasons

"Two are better than one, because they have a good return for their labour: If either of them falls down, one can help the other up."
— Ecclesiastes 4:9-10

The Journey of Intimacy

Marriage is a journey through seasons—joyful beginnings filled with promise, challenging middles marked by trials, and periods of change, grief, success, or transition. Each season brings its own rhythm, yet the constant thread that holds couples together is emotional connection and intimacy. These are the glue that binds hearts, allowing love to endure beyond circumstances.

Without deliberate effort, however, distance can quietly grow. Hearts may grow cold, and marriages can become vulnerable to drift and hardness. Intimacy does not sustain itself; it must be nurtured with care and intention.

Maintaining intimacy requires awareness of one another's needs, intentionality in daily choices, and a deep commitment to love, listen, and walk together both spiritually and emotionally. When couples embrace this posture, they discover that intimacy is not fragile but resilient, capable of carrying them through every season of life with tenderness and strength.

Intimacy: The Lifeblood of Marriage

Intimacy is the lifeblood of marriage. It is more than physical closeness; it is a sacred expression of covenant love that binds husband and wife together in body, soul, and spirit. Physical intimacy communicates desire, tenderness, and affection, reinforcing trust and protecting the marriage from external temptations. Spiritual intimacy, equally vital, is cultivated through prayer, worship, and seeking God's guidance together. When couples share spiritual vision and align their hearts with His design, they invite His presence to sustain their unity.

Yet when intimacy is neglected, the marriage bond begins to weaken across every dimension. Emotionally, affection fades and vulnerability diminish, leaving partners feeling rejected or alone. Relationally, distance grows, resentment festers, and communication falters. Spiritually, the covenant is strained, and as Paul warns in 1 Corinthians 7:5, withholding intimacy opens the door to temptation and spiritual vulnerability. Even physically, the absence of intimacy creates stress and tension, reminding us that body and soul are inseparably connected. A marriage without intimacy risks becoming two parallel lives rather than a shared covenant journey.

One of the greatest threats to intimacy is unforgiveness. When wounds remain unresolved, hearts grow hardened, trust is poisoned, and vulnerability is blocked.

Emotional distance spills into physical distance—touch loses tenderness, affection feels forced, and sexual connection becomes strained or absent. A hardened heart resists openness, turning closeness into duty rather than joy. As Jesus said, "Because of the hardness of your hearts…" (Matthew 19:8), couples drift from God's design, resisting the Spirit who brings tenderness, unity, and joy.

But restoration is always possible. Forgiveness clears resentment, humility softens hearts, and prayer rekindles tenderness.

Small acts of affection rebuild trust, and intimacy becomes sacred again—a reflection of God's faithfulness.

When hearts grow hard, intimacy grows cold; but forgiveness is the oxygen of marital love. It reopens trust, rekindles desire, and transforms sex into more than pleasure—it becomes healing, reconciliation, and renewal of covenant.

The impact of forgiveness is profound. Bitterness erodes affection, but forgiveness restores safety, the soil where passion flourishes. In a forgiving marriage, intimacy is not just physical—it is proof that love can rise again after conflict. Couples who practice forgiveness model resilience for their children and community, showing that love is not perfect, but it endures. A hardened heart starves intimacy, but forgiveness feeds it. In marriage, forgiveness is not only spiritual—it is sensual, practical, and essential for a love that lasts.

A Story of Navigating Life's Seasons

Consider Naomi and Elijah. Over twenty years of marriage, they experienced many seasons—the excitement of early marriage and career growth, the challenges of parenthood with sleepless nights and constant stress, the weight of financial pressures and extended family struggles, and the sorrow of personal losses coupled with spiritual testing. Each season carried its own trials, and without intentional practices, the stress could easily have driven them apart.

Yet Naomi and Elijah chose to protect their emotional connection with deliberate care. They made time for daily check-ins, even if only ten minutes during busy days. They committed to weekly date nights, refusing to let life's chaos steal their intimacy. They engaged in open conversations about emotions, fears, and desires, ensuring that silence never built walls between them.

Most importantly, they pursued spiritual alignment through prayer, fasting, and Bible study, anchoring their marriage in God's presence.

By embracing these practices, their intimacy deepened through every season. What could have fractured their bond instead strengthened it, and their love became resilient, enduring, and firmly rooted in God's design.

Lessons from Naomi and Elijah

Naomi and Elijah's marriage shows that resilience is not born out of ease but out of intentional choices. They learned that emotional connection must be protected daily, even in the midst of busyness or hardship. By carving out time for one another, they demonstrated that intimacy thrives when couples refuse to let life's demands overshadow their covenant.

Their story also reveals the power of consistency. Small practices—like brief daily check-ins, regular date nights, and honest conversations—may seem simple, but over time they build a strong foundation of trust and tenderness. Spiritual alignment was equally vital; prayer, fasting, and scripture study anchored their marriage in God's presence, ensuring that their love was not only emotional but deeply spiritual.

Through these disciplines, Naomi and Elijah discovered that intimacy can deepen through every season. Their marriage became a testimony that love, when nurtured intentionally, grows resilient and remains firmly rooted in God's design.

Understanding Emotional and Spiritual Connection

Intimacy is not just physical—it encompasses emotional bonding, spiritual alignment, physical expression, and relational rituals.

Emotional bonding involves sharing feelings, fears, and joys with openness, listening without judgment, and expressing empathy and care. These practices create a safe space where vulnerability is met with compassion, strengthening the heart-to-heart connection between spouses.

Spiritual alignment is equally vital. Couples who pray together, study God's Word together, and encourage one another in spiritual growth cultivate a shared sense of purpose and covenantal unity. This alignment anchors the marriage in God's design, ensuring that love is sustained not only by emotion but by faith.

Physical expression reinforces intimacy through affectionate touch, hugs, and closeness. Love is expressed in ways that are meaningful to each spouse, with physical intimacy serving as a natural extension of emotional and spiritual connection.

Relational rituals provide rhythm and consistency. Daily, weekly, and seasonal practices—such as celebrations, shared projects, and spiritual milestones—reinforce connection and remind couples of the covenant they are building together. These rituals transform ordinary moments into sacred opportunities to nurture love and unity.

Practical Steps to Maintain Connection Through Life's Seasons

Connection in marriage is sustained through intentional practices that nurture love and unity. Couples can begin by scheduling time together, even if it is only fifteen minutes of focused conversation or prayer each day.

Regular date nights or shared activities bring joy and closeness, reminding spouses that their relationship deserves priority amidst life's demands.

Open communication about life changes is equally vital. Sharing fears, stress, or concerns before they harden into silence prevents emotional distance. Expressing appreciation for each other's efforts during challenging seasons reinforces encouragement and strengthens resilience.

Celebrating milestones such as anniversaries, achievements, and spiritual victories adds rhythm and joy to the marriage. These celebrations cultivate gratitude and remind couples of the blessings they share.

Protecting the spiritual foundation of the relationship is essential. Praying together during stressful seasons and studying scripture to guide decisions keeps the marriage anchored in covenantal truth and builds spiritual resilience.

Finally, emotional responsiveness ensures that hearts remain tender. Validating your spouse's feelings, even in moments of disagreement, demonstrates empathy and care.

Consistent patience and encouragement create an atmosphere where love can thrive, even in the midst of trials.

Guarding Hearts, Nurturing Intimacy

Marriage is sustained not by chance but by covenantal devotion and intentional practices that keep hearts tender. When couples guard their hearts spiritually, emotionally, and relationally, intimacy proves resilient, able to endure both joy and trial. Transparency, vigilance, and consistent love form a bond that withstands every season.

By nurturing connection, aligning spiritually, and celebrating love daily, marriage becomes a living testimony of God's design. Soft hearts cultivate unity and trust, while hardened hearts invite distance and division.

To guard the heart is to protect intimacy, preserve covenant, and strengthen resilience.

A marriage flourishes when couples walk together with awareness, intentionality, and obedience to God, building not only a strong bond but a lasting legacy of love, unity, and faithfulness that endures through all seasons of life.

Illustrations of Sustained Intimacy

Grace and Michael faced the challenges of relocation and job stress, yet they chose to commit to nightly prayer and intentional check-ins. Despite the pressures of career changes, their emotional and spiritual intimacy deepened, proving that consistency in connection can transform seasons of strain into opportunities for growth.

Hannah and Peter navigated the difficulties of parenting teenagers, a season filled with frustrations and constant challenges. By openly sharing their struggles, praying together, and celebrating even the smallest victories, they maintained a united front. Their willingness to remain transparent and supportive protected their emotional connection and strengthened their bond as partners and parents.

Lydia and Samuel endured the pain of losing a loved one. Rather than allowing grief to create distance, they intentionally mourned together, prayed, and leaned on God's promises. In doing so, they turned a season of sorrow into one of closeness, allowing their faith and unity to carry them through loss without drifting apart.

Prophetic Insight

God designed marriage to thrive in every season. Emotional and spiritual intimacy anchors hearts in His covenant, keeping them soft and aligned.

Couples who remain connected through both joy and trial embody faith and resilience, inviting God's blessing.
The principle is simple: marriages that intentionally nurture intimacy reflect His love and faithfulness, becoming living testimonies of unity, strength, and enduring grace.

Reflection Exercises

Begin by identifying the current season of your marriage. Consider whether there are pressures or changes that may be threatening your emotional connection, and bring those realities into the light together. Awareness of the season you are in allows you to respond with intentional care rather than drift into distance.

Commit to one intentional practice this week that will deepen intimacy. Whether it is prayer, a date night, meaningful conversation, or a shared activity, let this practice become a deliberate act of love that strengthens your bond.

Take time to discuss openly with your spouse what helps each of you feel emotionally and spiritually connected. Honest dialogue about needs and desires creates understanding and prevents silence from building walls between you.

Finally, pray together, asking God to strengthen your bond through this season. Invite His Spirit to guard your hearts, soften your spirits, and reinforce the covenant that holds your marriage together.

Prayer

Lord, help us remain connected through every season of life. Protect our emotional, spiritual, and physical intimacy. Teach us to celebrate, support, and love each other consistently. Let our marriage reflect Your covenantal love, regardless of life's changes. Amen.

Declaration

"Our hearts remain united through every season. Emotional, spiritual, and physical connection flows continuously. Hardness, distance, and drift have no place in our marriage. We thrive together in love, grace, and covenantal faithfulness."

CHAPTER 14

Walking in Forgiveness: The Key to Eternal Softness of Heart

"Be kind to one another, tender hearted, forgiving one another, as God in Christ forgave you." — Ephesians 4:32

Forgiveness is the lifeblood of a tender heart in marriage. Without it, resentment begins to take root, emotional walls rise, and hearts grow hard. Jesus warned in Matthew 19:8 that hardness of heart is the root of relational collapse, reminding us that the refusal to forgive is not merely a personal choice but a spiritual danger. Walking in forgiveness is therefore essential to preserve intimacy, trust, and covenantal alignment with God.

Forgiveness is not optional—it is both a divine command and a covenantal safeguard. It releases hearts from the weight of offense, restores emotional and spiritual connection, and creates fertile ground for God's love to flow freely within the marriage. When couples choose forgiveness, they choose life, tenderness, and resilience. They invite God's Spirit to heal wounds, soften hearts, and strengthen the bond that no trial can sever.

A Story of Forgiveness Restoring Marriage

Consider the marriage of Naomi and David. Years into their union, repeated offenses and misunderstandings began to create growing distance. Naomi held onto past hurts, replaying them in her mind, while David, feeling unappreciated, became defensive and withdrawn. Emotional walls rose between them, threatening the very foundation of their marriage.

Through prayer and spiritual counsel, Naomi and David began a conscious journey of forgiveness. Naomi chose to release offense daily, asking God to soften her heart. David sought to make amends and committed himself to transparent communication. Together, they turned to scripture, immersing themselves in God's mercy, grace, and forgiveness.

Gradually, their hearts softened. Emotional intimacy returned, and the walls that once divided them crumbled. What had been a season of distance transformed into renewal, and their marriage was restored to vibrancy and spiritual alignment with God's covenant.

Understanding Forgiveness in Marriage

Forgiveness in marriage is more than words—it is a posture of the heart. It begins with the acknowledgment of offense, a willingness to recognise the hurt without justifying or dismissing it. This honesty allows wounds to be named so they can be healed.

From there, forgiveness requires the release of bitterness. Resentment cannot be carried forward without damaging intimacy, so couples must choose to let go of offense and refuse to allow it to harden their hearts.

Choosing to love despite offense is the next step. Love in marriage is not merely an emotion but an act of the will, a decision to remain faithful and tender even when feelings are strained.

Finally, forgiveness calls for seeking and offering reconciliation. This means taking intentional steps to restore trust, rebuild closeness, and invite emotional and spiritual unity back into the relationship.

When practiced in this way, forgiveness becomes a covenantal safeguard, protecting the marriage from drift and aligning it with God's design for lasting intimacy and resilience.

Spiritual Perspective

Forgiveness aligns hearts with God's covenantal design, opening the way for His grace to heal and sustain the marriage. When couples choose forgiveness, they are not simply resolving conflict—they are stepping into obedience to God's Word and allowing His Spirit to soften their hearts. Forgiveness dismantles walls of resentment, restores intimacy, and creates fertile ground for love to flourish.

Scripture reminds us of this truth: "Be kind and compassionate to one another, forgiving each other, just as in Christ God forgave you" (Ephesians 4:32). In marriage, this command becomes a safeguard against hardness of heart. By releasing offense and extending grace, couples mirror the forgiveness they themselves have received from God.

Forgiveness is therefore both a spiritual discipline and a covenantal safeguard. It keeps the marriage aligned with God's design, protects intimacy from erosion, and invites His blessing to rest upon the union. Where forgiveness flows, love is renewed, trust is restored, and God's presence sustains the bond through every season.

The Consequences of Unforgiveness

Unforgiveness in marriage carries devastating consequences. When offenses are left unresolved, emotional withdrawal and silence begin to take root, creating distance between hearts. Arguments escalate more quickly, defensiveness rises, and bitterness and resentment build layer upon layer, forming walls that are difficult to tear down. Over time, these patterns harden the heart, inviting relational drift and weakening the covenant bond that God designed to be tender and enduring.

Beyond the emotional toll, unforgiveness opens the door to spiritual vulnerability. A marriage that refuses to release offense becomes susceptible to attacks on its covenant, as mistrust and division replace unity and peace. Jesus' words in Matthew 19:8 remind us that hardness of heart is the root of relational collapse, and unforgiveness is one of the primary causes of that hardening.

When couples choose not to forgive, they risk losing intimacy, trust, and spiritual alignment. But when they embrace forgiveness, they invite God's healing presence to restore tenderness, protect their covenant, and sustain their love through every season.

Practical Steps to Walk in Forgiveness

Walking in forgiveness begins with a daily commitment to release offenses as soon as they occur. This choice prevents bitterness from taking root and keeps the heart tender. Prayer becomes essential in this process, as asking God to soften the heart ensures that forgiveness flows from His strength rather than human effort.

Forgiveness must also be communicated clearly. Verbally affirming that you forgive and desire reconciliation brings healing to the relationship. Avoiding reminders of past offenses allows the focus to remain on present restoration rather than reopening old wounds.

Seeking understanding is another vital step. Inviting your spouse to share their perspective and listening empathetically validates their intentions and struggles. This practice nurtures compassion and prevents miscommunication from becoming barriers to intimacy.

Grace must be extended generously. Forgiving fully, even when an apology has not yet been offered, reflects the example of Christ, who forgave freely and without condition.

True grace flows from God's mercy, not human merit, and couples who embrace this truth discover deeper unity.

Finally, forgiveness must be reinforced through actions. Trust is rebuilt through consistent, loving behaviour, and opportunities for reconnection—whether emotional closeness or spiritual alignment—restore the bond that unforgiveness once threatened. In this way, forgiveness becomes not only a spoken word but a lived reality that sustains intimacy and covenantal strength.

Illustrations of Forgiveness Restoring Hearts

Rachel and Daniel carried long-standing misunderstandings that had slowly eroded their closeness. Yet through intentional forgiveness and open dialogue, they chose to dismantle the walls between them. Emotional intimacy was restored, their hearts remained tender, and their marriage grew stronger and more resilient, proving that forgiveness can transform even the most entrenched struggles.

Hannah discovered the power of forgiveness as a daily practice. By choosing to release small irritations each day, her heart gradually softened. Patience replaced frustration, conflict diminished, and her marriage was strengthened by the steady rhythm of grace. What began as small acts of forgiveness became a lifestyle that nurtured peace and unity.

Lydia and Samuel sought spiritual restoration by praying daily for one another, asking God to remove offense and bitterness.

Their prayers opened the way for tenderness to return, emotional connection to deepen, and spiritual alignment to flourish. In choosing forgiveness, they invited God's presence to heal their hearts and renew their covenant.

Prophetic Insight

Marriage reflects God's forgiving and restorative love. When couples walk in forgiveness, walls crumble, trust is renewed, and hearts remain tender. Forgiveness deepens spiritual alignment, invites God's presence, and strengthens the covenant, making marriage resilient through every season. A soft heart draws grace, restores intimacy, and safeguards unity, ensuring love remains vibrant and enduring.

Reflection Exercises

Begin by identifying one unresolved offense that you may still be holding in your heart. Bring it before God in prayer and commit to releasing it today through verbal forgiveness, allowing His Spirit to soften what has grown heavy.

Take time to discuss openly with your spouse any areas where past offenses may still be affecting trust or intimacy. Honest dialogue creates space for healing and prevents hidden wounds from quietly eroding connection.

Establish a rhythm of forgiveness as a daily or weekly practice. Pray together for soft hearts and emotional restoration, inviting God to continually renew your bond and protect it from bitterness.

Finally, reflect on God's mercy toward you and allow it to become the model for extending forgiveness to your spouse. As you mirror His grace, your marriage will be strengthened, intimacy restored, and your covenant safeguarded against drift.

Prayer

Lord, teach us to forgive as You forgive. Remove all bitterness, resentment, and pride from our hearts. Help us extend grace, reconcile with love, and maintain tender, soft hearts in our marriage. Amen.

Declaration

"We walk in forgiveness daily. Hardness, offense, and resentment have no place in our hearts or marriage. Our hearts remain tender, our love flows freely, and our marriage thrives in unity, grace, and covenantal faithfulness."

CHAPTER 15

Walking in Covenant Love: Living the Design for a Lifetime

"Let love and faithfulness never leave you; bind them around your neck, write them on the tablet of your heart."
— Proverbs 3:3

Covenant Love: The Blueprint for Lifelong Marital Success

Covenant love is the ultimate expression of God's design for marriage. It is not fleeting emotion or conditional affection, but a lifelong commitment rooted in faith, obedience, and spiritual alignment with Him. This love is steadfast, enduring through seasons of joy and seasons of trial, sustaining the marriage when circumstances shift and life's pressures mount. Covenant love heals wounded hearts, prevents drift, and ensures that intimacy, trust, and unity remain strong.

This chapter brings together the essential principles that safeguard and strengthen marriage: the softening of hearts to resist hardness, the practice of forgiveness that restores tenderness, the cultivation of emotional connection that keeps love vibrant, and the daily spiritual disciplines that anchor the union in God's presence. Together, these practices form a comprehensive blueprint for lifelong marital success.

When couples embrace covenant love, they reflect God's faithfulness and embody His design for unity. Their marriage becomes not only a source of joy and resilience but also a living testimony of His grace, shining as a witness to the world of what love rooted in covenant can accomplish.

A Story of Covenant Love in Action

Consider the marriage of Ruth and Elijah. Over thirty years together, they experienced the excitement and trials of early marriage, navigated the challenges of parenting, career pressures, and extended family dynamics, and endured seasons marked by health issues, grief, and loss. They also faced spiritual testing and periods of distance that could have weakened their bond.

Yet through every season, Ruth and Elijah remained committed to covenant love. They prayed daily, spoke affirmations over one another, and studied scripture to keep their hearts aligned with God's truth. They pursued intentional emotional and spiritual connection, choosing forgiveness and grace whenever offense arose. They guarded their hearts against bitterness and pride, ensuring that tenderness and unity were preserved.

As a result, their marriage became a living testimony of steadfast covenant love. Their lifelong commitment proved that when aligned with God's design, marriage is not only possible but deeply fruitful, radiating resilience, intimacy, and faithfulness through every stage of life.

Closing Statement

Covenant love is a living testimony of God's faithfulness—enduring trials, healing wounds, and flourishing in joy. Rooted in grace and forgiveness, marriage becomes a prophetic witness that "Love never fails" (1 Corinthians 13:8), leaving a legacy of unity and hope for generations to come.

Affirmation

Covenant love endures every season, reflecting God's faithfulness and leaving a legacy of unity and grace.

Covenant Love

Covenant love is not shaped by fleeting emotions but anchored in God's eternal design and promises. It is a love that chooses faithfulness even when feelings falter, rooting marriage in divine truth rather than human impulse. Such love is resilient, fortified by grace, and able to endure both joy and hardship without breaking. It protects the heart from bitterness, nurtures intimacy, and shields the union from spiritual attack, preserving tenderness and unity. Above all, covenant love is purposeful—it reflects God's covenantal nature, bringing Him glory through every act of faithfulness, forgiveness, and intimacy. Marriage, then, is not merely human partnership but a divine calling.

Spiritual Perspective

To walk in covenant love is to live intentionally in alignment with God's blueprint, allowing His Spirit to shape every word, choice, and priority. This love is active, requiring deliberate obedience to God's design and a continual surrender to His guidance. When couples invite the Holy Spirit into their relationship, their marriage becomes a living testimony of grace, unity, and resilience. Scripture affirms this truth: "Therefore what God has joined together, let no one separate" (Mark 10:9). Marriage is sustained not by human effort alone but by God's presence, which guards hearts, directs paths, and strengthens bonds against trials. In this way, covenant love becomes more than a commitment between two people—it becomes a reflection of God's eternal covenant with His people, a witness of His mercy and steadfast love that endures through every season.

Living Covenant Love

Covenant love is a daily choice—faithfulness over feeling, devotion over drift.

It thrives when couples pray together, seek God's Word, and invite His Spirit into every decision.

Tenderness grows through affirmation, touch, and shared joy, while vigilance guards against pride, offense, and division.

Grace and forgiveness keep hearts soft, dissolving walls and renewing trust.

And beyond the present, covenant love builds legacy—marriage as a testimony of God's design, blessing generations with unity, strength, and enduring faithfulness.

Illustrations of Covenant Love

Lydia and Samuel endured seasons of financial strain and health crises that could have easily fractured their bond. Yet by prioritising covenant love, they chose to support one another emotionally and spiritually. Their steadfast devotion carried them through hardship, and they emerged stronger, more united, and deeply anchored in God's design for marriage.

Hannah and Peter discovered the power of daily commitment. Through affirmations, prayer, and intentional gestures of love, they reinforced their covenantal devotion. Even in stressful seasons, these practices prevented drift and kept their hearts tender, proving that consistent acts of love sustain intimacy and resilience.

Ruth and Elijah's over three decades marriage considered earlier, became a living legacy. Their steadfast covenantal love not only strengthened their own union but also served as a model for their children and community. Their faithfulness inspired generations, glorifying God and demonstrating that covenant love is both enduring and transformative.

Reflection Exercises

Commit each day to one intentional act of covenant love—through prayer, affirmation, or service—as a tangible expression of devotion. Reflect on your marriage covenant and record practical ways to live it daily, anchoring your relationship in consistent, purposeful choices. Engage in honest conversation with your spouse to strengthen spiritual, emotional, and physical connection, fostering deeper intimacy and unity. Finally, pray together, inviting God's Spirit to guard your union, renew your hearts, and sustain your covenant through every season.

Prayer

Lord, help us walk in covenant love all our days. Strengthen our hearts, minds, and spirits to remain tender, forgiving, and committed. Let our marriage reflect Your covenantal faithfulness and bring glory to Your name. Amen.

Declaration

"We walk in covenant love daily. Our hearts are tender, our trust unshaken, and our intimacy flows continually. Hardness, bitterness, and drift have no place in our marriage. We live God's design for a lifetime, leaving a legacy of love, faith, and unity."

CHAPTER 16

Love, Truth, and the Healing of Hearts

Marriage is not sustained by vows alone, but by hearts that remain tender before God and to one another. Intimacy—physical, emotional, and spiritual—is the lifeblood of covenant love. Yet unforgiveness hardens hearts, erodes trust, and starves intimacy. Hardness of heart is the hidden enemy of marriage. It erects walls where God designed for bridges, turning love into duty and intimacy into silence.

But forgiveness is the weapon that tears down those walls. Forgiveness reopens trust, rekindles desire, and restores joy. It transforms sex from a mechanical act into reconciliation, prayer into partnership, and daily life into testimony. When couples choose humility over pride, tenderness over resentment, and prayer over silence, they rediscover the covenant God intended. Homes become sanctuaries of love, unity, and strength. Children witness resilience, communities see hope, and generations inherit a legacy of faith.

This is the call of Matthew 19:8: to resist hardness of heart and embrace God's design. Marriage is not fragile—it is a divine covenant, empowered by grace and sustained by love. It is a living parable of Christ and His Church; a testimony that covenant commitment is not only possible but fruitful.

Yet healing never begins in silence—it begins when truth is finally given permission to speak. As Scripture declares in Psalm 51:6: "Surely You desire truth in the inner parts…" Truth has always been the place where God begins His deepest work. And often, the hardest truth to face is the one we already know—the cracks we've quietly stepped around, the distance that has slowly widened between us, the wounds we tucked away, hoping time alone would mend them.

This truth lingers beneath conversations, sits quietly in the room even when words never come, and whispers: "Something is hurting… but something can still be healed."

To embrace truth requires courage. It asks us to acknowledge what has been breaking, to confront what we've avoided, to admit that love cannot heal what we refuse to face. Yet truth—when welcomed—does not come to shame or divide. It comes to soften hearts, open understanding, and give relationships the room to breathe again. Truth clears the fog. Truth melts the hardness. Truth invites us back into honesty, vulnerability, and connection.

Real healing does not wait for perfection. It begins the moment we surrender from hiding, lay down the pretending, release the emotional distance, and finally give God space to restore what has been wounded. This is the door before you now—the door of truth, courage, mercy, and healing.

Relationships do not survive on silence. They survive on truth—spoken in love, received in humility, and carried out with grace. When husbands and wives choose forgiveness over bitterness, tenderness over distance, and prayer over silence, they become witnesses of God's faithfulness. Their love becomes a sermon louder than words, a testimony that covenant love can endure storms and emerge stronger.

Your marriage is more than survival—it is meant to flourish. Flourishing marriages inspire children to believe in love, encourage communities to value covenant, and leave a generational legacy of faith. This is the inheritance God desires for His people: homes filled with His presence, relationships marked by resilience, and love that reflects eternity.

Healing is not a single act—it is a journey. Some days will feel lighter, others heavier, but every step forward is a step toward wholeness. Let patience guide you through the delicate spaces. Let empathy soften your responses when old wounds resurface. And let God's presence be the constant in every conversation, every silence, and every pause between words.

The truth you have faced is not an ending—it is an invitation. An invitation to deeper love, greater intimacy, and a relationship that honours both your hearts and God's design.

So, walk boldly through this door—not in fear of what truth may reveal, but in faith that every revelation carries the seed of restoration.

Step forward in truth. Walk in grace. And let love—steadfast, tender, and unwavering—carry you into the fullness of what God intended from the beginning.

Closing Prayer

Heavenly Father, we thank You for the gift of marriage, designed as a covenant to reflect Your love for the Church. Where hearts have grown hard, soften them by Your Spirit. Where intimacy has been lost, restore tenderness, trust, and joy. Where unforgiveness has built walls, let Your grace tear them down and replace them with bridges of reconciliation.

Bless every couple who reads these words. May their homes become sanctuaries of love, unity, and strength. May their marriages flourish as testimonies of Your faithfulness, leaving a legacy of covenant love for generations to come.

In Jesus' name, Amen.

Acknowledgments

I give deepest thanks to God, whose wisdom and presence have guided every step of this work. He is the true source of covenant love and the life behind these words.

To my family, friends, and mentors who prayed, encouraged, and believed in this message, I dedicate this work with gratitude. Your support has been a constant strength and reminder that this calling is upheld by community.

To the couples and individuals whose stories embody resilience and covenant love, I offer reverence. Though fictional, their journeys reflect God's design for marriage and serve as living parables of steadfast love. May they inspire generations to embrace covenant commitment as both possible and fruitful.

Recommended Reading

1. *The Meaning of Marriage* by Timothy Keller
2. *Love & Respect* by Emerson Eggerichs
3. *The 5 Love Languages* by Gary Chapman
4. *Sacred Marriage* by Gary Thomas
5. *Marriage God's Way* by Scott LaPierre

About the Author

Mike Olorogun is a Christian teacher, mentor, and author with a passion for restoring marriages through God's Word. He believes marriage is a divine covenant, not just a social contract, and speaks with clarity and compassion to couples facing drift, wounds, or hardened hearts.

Blending scripture, prophetic insight, and practical wisdom accumulated in over three decades, Mike equips intending couples, husbands and wives with tools for communication, forgiveness, and spiritual partnership. His vision is to see homes transformed into sanctuaries of love, unity, and generational legacy.

His earlier books include *Think Before You Say "I Do"*, *Now That You Are Married*, and *Marriages in Distress.*

Mike is happily married with children, and they reside in both the United Kingdom and the United States of America.

ABOUT THE BOOK

When Hearts Grow Hard: The Hidden Reason Marriages Break Down — Healing the Heart Through Matthew 19:8

Marriage was designed by God as a lifelong covenant, yet too many unions collapse quietly—eroded by emotional distance, spiritual drift, and unhealed wounds. In this compassionate and prophetic guide, Mike Olorogun uncovers the root cause of marital breakdown: hardness of heart.

With biblical wisdom, vivid illustrations, and practical steps, this book equips couples to:

- Recognise the subtle signs of emotional and spiritual disconnection
- Heal wounded hearts and rebuild trust through forgiveness
- Restore intimacy—emotional, spiritual, and physical
- Navigate conflict and external pressures with grace and resilience
- Build a marriage that thrives and leaves a lasting legacy

When Hearts Grow Hard is more than a book—it is a roadmap to covenant love. Whether you are seeking to prevent divorce, restore a struggling marriage, or strengthen an already healthy relationship, this work offers hope, clarity, and spiritual insight to transform your union into a living testimony of God's faithfulness.

Your marriage is not destined to merely survive—it can flourish, inspire, and become a generational sanctuary of love and strength.

www.ingramcontent.com/pod-product-compliance
Lightning Source LLC
LaVergne TN
LVHW020511100826
845148LV00003B/757

* 9 7 8 9 7 8 6 8 0 7 9 0 4 *